"With courage and tenderness President Phil Ryken tells Wheaton College students that no college needs the gospel more than Wheaton College. It's not that the sins of Wheaton students are greater than those of others, but rather that their need of grace for godly power and peace is no less. In a college culture where you are expected to be holy and smart and successful, President Ryken teaches students (and the rest of us) not only that grace is greater than all our sin but also that it is release from human pressures and fuel for fruitful joy."

Bryan Chapell, author, *Holiness by Grace*; Chancellor, Covenant Theological Seminary

"'Cheer up! God's grace is greater than you can imagine.' Whether you're a novice or a veteran in the school of grace, these words are meant to refresh, enliven and illumine your heart. I'm so thankful for Ryken's bold yet humble declaration of the marvelous grace of God— grace meant for all who believe, grace that is ours from the beginning of our walk all the way into the eternity we're longing for. Pick up this lovely little book and let its ageless message remind you of the grace that first transformed your soul."

Elyse Fitzpatrick, counselor; speaker; author, *Give Them Grace* and *Comforts from the Cross*

"Phil Ryken's *Grace Transforming* is a captivating series of chapel addresses reminding us that we never outgrow our need for the transforming power of God's grace. With wonderful illustrations, sound biblical exegesis, and hard-hitting, relevant applications, Phil invites us to face the realities of our own life in order to realize in ever more profound ways the power of God's life-changing grace. I was personally enriched by reading this new treasure and reminded of the things I love the most, even when I fail to realize their lively, pulsating reality in my own life."

Gayle D. Beebe, President, Westmont College; author, *The Shaping of an Effective Leader* and *Longing for God*

"Hebrews 13:9 says, 'It is good for the heart to be strengthened by grace.' As a church planter, I needed the truths in this book to strengthen my weary, performance-driven, approval-hungry, externally oriented, and self-righteous heart. My pharisaical heart was exposed, and I found myself praying, 'God, be mercy-seated to me, the sinner.'"

David Choi, Lead Planter, Church of the Beloved, Chicago, Illinois; International Speaker

"To grasp the fullness of God's grace is to come humbly to Christ in empty-handed spiritual poverty. That alone may be the greatest challenge for any Christian! And it's why I so appreciate Phil Ryken's extraordinary insights in this new book. He points us to Jesus Christ in all his saving power, reminding us that without the Savior we are nothing and have nothing. If you are seeking a fresh look at your Lord and your own desperate need of him, this is the book for you!"

Joni Eareckson Tada, Joni and Friends International Disability Center

"I listened attentively in chapel during every one of Dr. Ryken's messages and found them life-giving, and I'm sure I'll need it for the rest of my life. The grace of Christ is so simple yet so hard to fathom. Ryken illuminates the power of grace, combining artful prose, inspiring quotations, and personal anecdotes. Here's a book that hands readers transforming grace on a silver platter."

T. Ryan Buchanan, 2011 Student Body President, Wheaton College; Teach for America Corps member

GRACE

transforming

PHIL RYKEN

ivp

INTER-VARSITY PRESS
Norton Street, Nottingham NG7 3HR, England
Email: ivp@ivpbooks.com
Website: www.ivpbooks.com

First published 2012

British Library Cataloguing in Publication Data
A catalogue record for this book is available from the British Library.

ISBN: 978-1-84474-606-4

Typeset in the United States of America
Printed and bound in Great Britain by the MPG Books Group

*Inter-Varsity Press publishes Christian books that are true to the Bible and that
communicate the gospel, develop discipleship and strengthen the church for its
mission in the world.*

*Inter-Varsity Press is closely linked with the Universities and Colleges Christian
Fellowship, a student movement connecting Christian Unions in universities and
colleges throughout Great Britain, and a member movement of the International
Fellowship of Evangelical Students. Website: www.uccf.org.uk*

To the students of Wheaton College,
whose friendship is a
gift of God's grace.

CONTENTS

PREFACE

This book began as a series of chapel messages given at Wheaton College. Wheaton is a performance-oriented place, so in my first year as president I wanted to speak as often as I could about the grace of God. Instead of being defined by who we are and what we do, we are defined by who Jesus is and what he has done for us in his death and resurrection.

I am grateful to Crossway for the invitation to edit my chapel messages on God's life-changing grace and adapt them for a wider audience. I am also grateful to Marilee Melvin for her help in making many corrections to the original manuscript.

Our family has been deeply grateful for the extraordinary welcome we have received from the Wheaton College community, especially the students. Their friendship and openness to God's work in their lives make it a joy to teach them the Word of God. This book is sent to press with gratitude to God for the high privilege of serving as their president.

Phil Ryken
Wheaton, Illinois

1

GRACE'S HUMBLING NECESSITY

We begin at the beginning, with our desperate need for grace. From the moment we came into the world as helpless babies, right up until this exact second, we are utterly and completely dependent on the grace of God for everything we have, including life itself. What is more, if we have any hope of life after death—eternal life—it is only because of God's free and undeserved grace for us in Jesus Christ.

Until we understand this, it is impossible for us to have the relationship with God that we truly need. But when we do understand this—when we understand our absolute need for Jesus—then his grace changes everything.

PAST EXPERIENCE, PRESENT NEED

Our need for grace may seem obvious at the beginning of the Christian life, when we first put our trust in Jesus. Then we know that if there is anything we contribute to our salvation, it is only the sin that necessitates a Savior. According to the good news of our salvation, Jesus died and rose again so that in him we would receive forgiveness for our sins and enter into everlasting fellowship with the true and living God. We are not saved by anything that we have done, therefore, but only by what Jesus has done. It is all by his grace, not by our works.

Yet grace is not something we leave behind once we decide to follow Jesus. Grace is our present need as well as our past experience. The gospel is not just the way *into* the Christian life; it is also the way *on in* the Christian life. We continually need to remember that God "saved us and called us to a holy calling, not because of our works but because of his own purpose and grace, which he gave us in Christ Jesus" (2 Tim. 1:9).

In my first chapel address as president of Wheaton College I said something that took some people by surprise, maybe because it's something that many Christians forget. I said that I don't know of a college anywhere in the world that needs the gospel more than Wheaton does.

In saying this, I did not mean to imply that there aren't a lot of Christians at Wheaton. In fact, every student, every professor, and every staff member on campus makes a personal profession of faith in Jesus Christ. Still, it wouldn't be surprising to find unbelievers on campus: in most Christian communities there are at least some people who do not yet have a saving relationship with Jesus Christ.

This is not what I meant, however, when I said that Wheaton College needs the gospel. I meant that the gospel is for Christians every bit as much as it is for non-Christians. We never outgrow our need for God's life-changing grace— the gospel of the cross and the empty tomb.

A SELF-CENTERED PRAYER

The main reason we continue to need the gospel is that we continue to sin. To experience God's life-changing grace for ourselves, therefore, we need to recognize the deep-seated sin that necessitates our salvation.

One of the best places to see our need for grace, and also the way that God answers that need, is in a story Jesus told "to some who trusted in themselves that they were righteous, and treated others with contempt" (Luke 18:9). In other words, this is a story for people who will not admit their need for grace. It is a story for us, if we are too proud to confess our sins. It goes like this:

> Two men went up into the temple to pray, one a Pharisee and the other a tax collector. The Pharisee, standing by himself, prayed thus: "God, I thank you that I am not like other men, extortioners, unjust, adulterers, or even like this tax collector. I fast twice a week; I give tithes of all that I get." But the tax collector, standing far off, would not even lift up his eyes to heaven, but beat his breast, saying, "God, be merciful to me, a sinner!" I tell you, this man went down to his house justified, rather than the other. For everyone who exalts himself will be humbled, but the one who humbles himself will be exalted. (Luke 18:10–14)

15

The story opens with a surprise, because in those days everyone knew that tax collectors did not go to the temple and did not pray. Tax collectors were employed by the Roman government, and thus they were considered traitors to the Jewish people. Many practiced extortion. Thus one preacher compared them to "drug pushers and pimps, those who prey on society, and make a living of stealing from others."[1] Make no mistake about it: this tax collector was a crook!

The Pharisee, by contrast, stood for everything that was right and good. The Pharisees were widely regarded as spiritual overachievers. They were theologically orthodox and morally devout. Possibly our respect for this particular Pharisee increases when we overhear his prayer. He comes before God with thanksgiving. He testifies that he is not an extortioner or an adulterer. Rather than taking money for himself, he gives it away to others. He not only prays, but also fasts. In contemporary terms, this man would be a pastor or a theologian—or maybe the president of a Christian college.

Yet for all his devotion, the Pharisee was not righteous in the sight of God. Why not? His most obvious problem was pride. Although he began by addressing God, he spent the rest of his prayer talking about himself. In only two short verses he manages to mention himself five (!) times: I . . . I . . . I . . . I . . . I. It gets worse, because if we translate verse 11 more literally, it reads, "The Pharisee, standing, prayed *about* himself," or even *"with* himself," in which case he was not talking to God at all! He did not truly ask God for anything or offer God any praise but simply reveled in his own sense of moral superiority. In other words, the Pharisee was exactly like the people listening to Jesus tell this story: confident of his own righteousness. Here is a man, said London's famous preacher Charles Spurgeon, who thought he was "too good to be saved."[2]

It is easy to see how self-righteous the Pharisee was, but what we really need to assess is the same attitude in ourselves. If we are living in Christian community, then either we will grow strong in the grace of God or else we will become bigger and bigger hypocrites. So we need to ask ourselves: When am I like the Pharisee in the story Jesus told?

Here are some possible answers: I am a Pharisee when I care more about my religious reputation than about real holiness. I am a Pharisee when I look down on people who are not as committed to the cause of mercy or justice that I am committed to. I am a Pharisee when I look around and say, "Thank God I am not like so-and-so" and then fill in the blank with whatever person in my neighborhood, or student on my campus, or colleague at my workplace, or family in my church, or group in my society that I happen to think is not as whatever it is as I am.

When else am I a Pharisee? I am a Pharisee when I am impressed with how much I am giving to God compared to others. I am a Pharisee when other people's sins seem worse than my own. I am a Pharisee when I can go all day, or all week, or even all month without confessing any particular sin.

ANOTHER WAY TO PRAY

Thankfully, there is a totally different way to pray—a way that will save your sinful and maybe hypocritical soul. Unlike the Pharisee, the tax collector did not count on his own merits but begged for mercy instead: "The tax collector, standing far off, would not even lift up his eyes to heaven, but beat his breast, saying, 'God, be merciful to me, a sinner!'" (Luke 18:13).

There are three parts to the tax collector's prayer: God, the sinner, and the merciful grace that comes between them. The man's prayer started with God, which is where all prayer ought to begin. The first act of prayer is to approach the majestic throne of the awesome and almighty God. When the tax collector made his approach, he refused even to look up to heaven, because he had a right and proper fear of God's bright, burning holiness.

So the tax collector's prayer began with God. It ended with himself, the sinner. I say "the" sinner, rather than "a" sinner because the Greek original of this verse uses the definite article. As far as the tax collector was concerned, he was the only sinner that mattered. Rather than comparing himself to others, he measured himself against the perfect holiness of God. And by that standard, he saw himself for what he was: nothing more and nothing less than a guilty sinner before a holy God.

Dietrich Bonhoeffer wisely wrote, "If my sinfulness appears to me to be in any way smaller or less detestable in comparison with the sins of others, I am still not recognizing my sinfulness at all."³ One good way to avoid this error and acknowledge the true extent of our sin is to identify ourselves as "the" sinner when we pray, as if we were the biggest, most obvious sinner in our congregation, corporation, family, or dormitory. "It's me, Lord," we should say when we begin our prayers. "You know: the sinner."

AT THE MERCY SEAT

This brings us to the most striking feature of the tax collector's prayer: in between God's holiness and his own sinfulness he inserted a prayer for mercy. Like King David, he stood before God and said, "Give ear, O LORD, to my prayer; listen to my plea for grace" (Ps. 86:6).

When the tax collector prayed, "Have mercy," he used a Greek verb that essentially means to atone for sin by means of a blood sacrifice. To understand this, we need to go back in the Old Testament to Leviticus 16. Once a year, the high priest would make atonement for the people's sin. He would take a perfect male goat and sacrifice it as a sin offering. Then he would take its blood into the Most Holy Place of the temple and sprinkle it on the mercy seat.

What did this priestly act signify? The sacrificial goat represented God's sinful people. In a symbolical way, their sins were transferred or imputed to the animal. Then, having been charged with sin, the animal was put to death. The goat thus served as a substitute, dying in the place of sinners.

Once a sacrifice had been offered, the animal's blood was the proof that atonement had been made for sin. The sacrificial blood showed that God had already carried out his death penalty against transgression. So the priest took the blood and sprinkled it on the mercy seat, which was the golden lid on the ark of the covenant. This sacred ark was located in the innermost sanctum of the temple—the Most Holy Place. On top of the mercy seat there were golden cherubim, symbolizing the throne of God. Thus the ark served as the earthly location of God's holy presence. Inside the ark, underneath the mercy seat, was the law of God as a covenant that the people had broken. Sprinkling blood on the mercy seat, therefore, was a way to show that an atoning sacrifice had come between the holy God and his sinful people. The sacrificial blood showed that their sins were covered, that they were protected from the holy wrath of God.

In effect, this is what the tax collector prayed for when he said, "God, be merciful to me, the sinner." He was asking God to make blood atonement for his sin. There the man was, praying in the very temple where the sacrificial blood was sprinkled on the mercy seat. When Jesus says that "two men went up to the temple to pray," this is generally taken to mean that they were there around three o'clock in the afternoon, with the crowds that attended the daily sacrifice. Knowing that he was under God's judgment because of his sin, the only thing the tax collector could do was ask for mercy to come between his guilt and God's wrath. So he begged for God to be "mercy-seated" to him. He was asking God to atone for his sins, to cover his guilt, and to protect him from eternal judgment.

The order of the tax collector's prayer echoes the Old Testament pattern for sacrifice: "God, be merciful to me, the sinner." First comes God, who is perfect in his holiness. Last comes the sinner, who deserves to die for his sins. But in between comes the sacrificial blood that saves his sinful soul.

SAVED BY THE BLOOD

This is a good prayer for anyone to pray: "God, be mercy-seated to me, the sinner." Not counting the Lord's Prayer, or the words of thanks I give before eating a meal, it is probably the prayer I offer more than any other. It's short and easy to remember. I pray it first thing in the morning or the last thing at night. I pray it before I preach, or any time I am feeling weighed down by guilt: "God, be merciful to me, the sinner."

When I pray this way, I am really praying the gospel. By shedding his blood, Jesus Christ became the atoning sacrifice for my sins. His death is my substitute; his cross is my mercy seat; and the blood that he sprinkled on it is my salvation.

To say that Jesus died for sinners is to say that his sacrifice accomplished what the blood on the mercy seat accomplished. Like the sacrificial animals of the Old Testament, Jesus died in our place. Our sins were transferred or imputed to him: "He himself bore our sins in his body on the tree" (1 Pet. 2:24). As a result, our sins are covered; our guilt is taken away. The Scripture says Christ "has appeared once for all at the end of the ages to put away sin by the sacrifice of himself" (Heb. 9:26).

Our mercy seat is the cross of Jesus Christ, where the atoning blood was sprinkled for our salvation. In fact, to explain what Jesus was doing on the cross, the New Testament sometimes uses the noun form of the same verb for *mercy* that we find in Luke 1. We see this terminology in Romans 3:25, which says that God presented Jesus "as a propitiation by his blood," and again in Hebrews 2:17, where he is described as a "merciful and faithful high priest in the service of God," who has made "propitiation for the sins of the people."

This is mercy-seat vocabulary, which assures us that our plea for grace will always be answered. When we say, "God, be merciful to me, the sinner," we are making an appeal to the cross. We are asking for the blood of Jesus to cover all our sins.

GOING HOME JUSTIFIED

Has God been mercy-seated to you? What compels me to ask this question is the conclusion to the story Jesus told. Two men went to the temple, where they offered two different prayers and, as a result, met two entirely different destinies. In the end, the tax collector got what he asked for. His prayers were answered. God was mercy-seated to him. Thus Jesus closed his story by saying that this man (and not the other) was "justified." In other words— and we will say more about this in a later chapter—the tax collector was counted righteous. He was justified by God's mercy on the basis of the atoning blood of a perfect sacrifice, which he received by a prayer he asked in faith.

God did not justify the Pharisee, however. This would have come as a total shock to anyone who was listening to this story when it was first told, so Jesus was very specific about it. Although the Pharisee declared his own righteousness, he was never declared righteous by God, and therefore he went home *un*justified. Sadly, his righteousness was part of the problem. He was too busy being self-righteous to receive God's righteousness, which comes only as a gift.

The Pharisee's prayer was all about what he could do for God: "I thank . . . I am . . . I fast . . . I give." All his verbs were active, in the first person singular. What made the tax collector's prayer different was that he was asking God to do something for him. Therefore, the only verb in his prayer is passive: "God, be mercy-seated to me, the sinner."

23

Pray this way, and you too will be justified before God. What is more, you will be so humbled by your desperate need for God's life-changing grace that you will not look down on anyone but live instead with the humility, joy, and gratitude that only grace compels.

2

GRACE'S
COSTLY PROVISION

As Paul considered the economy of God in the incarnation of his Son, he noticed a staggering inequity. By the apostle's accounting, an extraordinary exchange had taken place—the largest transfer of wealth in human history. Here is how he described it: "For you know the grace of our Lord Jesus Christ, that though he was rich, yet for your sake he became poor, so that you by his poverty might become rich" (2 Cor. 8:9).

This simple verse is elegant in its structural perfection. It comes in the form that Bible scholars call "chiasm." There is a crossover or inversion, in which the second half of the verse reverses the order of the first: rich, poor, poor, rich. In the space of a single verse, Paul explains the true meaning of Christ's saving work, using the language of wealth and poverty to communicate the gospel. He also teaches us how to live, giving us all the motivation we ever need to spend our lives for the Savior, who spent his life for us.

Furthermore, Paul describes all of this as a demonstration of God's grace. Consider his words again: "For you know the *grace* of our Lord Jesus Christ, that though he was rich, yet for your sake he became poor, so that you by his poverty might become rich" (2 Cor. 8:9). This verse is about the costly provision of the grace of God.

THE RICHES OF THE SON

In describing God's costly provision of grace, Paul starts with the fabulous riches of the Son of God. So consider for a moment the vast wealth of the second person of the Trinity—the wealth he possessed before his incarnation, in his eternal preexistence as God the everlasting Son.

Paul calls Jesus "our Lord," reminding us of our personal relationship to Christ and of his supreme and absolute sovereignty. Before the Son of God became a man, he was the firstborn over all creation, the ruler of heaven and earth. By virtue of his authority and power, displayed in his creation of all things out of nothing, God the Son was the ruler of all nature. There was nothing in this entire universe that did not belong to him.

Yet, even for all their beauty, the glories of the galaxies could not compare with the opulent splendor of heaven itself. To understand the riches of the Son of God more fully, you would have to catch a glimpse of his royal majesty in the throne room of heaven. This majesty is beautifully expressed in an invitation from the medieval mystic Hildegard of Bingen:

Come, enter into the palace of the King.
O glittering light of the stars,
O most splendid one,
O unique beauty of royal wedding,
O shining gem:
You are adorned, O high personage
Without spot or blemish.[1]

If you were to enter the palace of that King—here I
am still talking about the time prior to his incarnation,
before God the Son became a man—you would have seen
what Isaiah witnessed when he saw "the Lord sitting
upon a throne, high and lifted up" (Isa. 6:1). John tells
us that when Isaiah saw this, he was witnessing the very
glory of Jesus Christ (John 12:41). There the prophet saw
angelic beings shining in holiness, the seraphim who
gather around the throne of God and chant, "Holy, holy,
holy is the LORD of hosts; the whole earth is full of his
glory" (Isa. 6:3).

Presumably these bright angels have been saying this
since the beginning of time. Endless adoration. Ceaseless
praise. This is all part of the riches of the Son of God.
Paul tells us in an offhand sort of way that we *know* the
riches that Christ possessed before he became a man, but
I wonder if we really do. He was so rich that his servants
were bright angels. Long before we were created, God
the Son existed in the perfect blessedness of his pristine
glory—the glory he had with the Father before the worlds
began (John 17:5).

THE POVERTY OF THE CHRIST

Yet he became poor. Here the economy of redemption takes a surprising turn, as the Christ undergoes a reversal of fortune.

The vast majority of Christians in the West have never experienced real poverty. Some of us have been to places in the world where people live in true poverty, and a few of us have lived among the poor. Yet most of our experience with poverty has been moderated by the certainty of our next meal, or the expectation of returning soon to more affluent surroundings. Our engagement with the poor is protected by our wealth.

I wonder how many of us would have the courage to give away everything we have—even if we knew that God was calling us to do it—and live in absolute poverty, utterly dependent on the daily provision of God.

This is what Jesus did when he divested himself of heaven's glory. I love the way this is expressed in a Christmas lyric by the English hymn writer Frank Houghton. The song begins like this: "Thou who wast rich beyond all splendor / All for love's sake becamest poor." Then it goes on to explain some of the riches that Jesus exchanged for poverty: "Thrones for a manger didst surrender / Sapphire-paved courts for stable floor."

The second stanza explains more specifically what Christ did to impoverish himself: "Thou who art God beyond all praising / All for love's sake becamest man." Compared to the glories of heaven, it was the very act of becoming a human being that plunged the Son of God into poverty. According to the rules of engagement that he adopted for his incarnation, he would not use his divine power for personal advantage but would suffer the difficulties of life in a fallen world. He would give up the glory of his deity—not his deity itself, but the glory of it—to take on our humanity with all its limitations.

But that is not all. His primary poverty was his very humanity, but within the wide range of economic circumstances in the ancient world—from peasants to kings—God sent his Son into a poor family.

The poverty of Mary and Joseph is demonstrated not so much in the stable where their son was born, which seems to have been an act of necessity, but in something that happened five weeks later. Luke 2:22 tells us that "when the time came for their purification according to the Law of Moses," Mary and Joseph took Jesus up to Jerusalem. Typically when a God-fearing family participated in the ritual for purification, they would give the priest a lamb to sacrifice as a burnt offering. But in his law God made special provision for the poor. According to Leviticus, if a woman "cannot afford a lamb, then she shall take two turtledoves" (Lev. 12:8). This is what Mary did, indicating that she and Joseph were in the lowest income bracket.

I love this purification story for what it tells us about God: he always makes provision for the poor, as we should also do. But I also love what it tells us about the Son of God: in becoming human, he did not insist on his royal prerogatives but made himself poor. "He did not avail himself of his right to make himself rich," said the old Princeton theologian Charles Hodge, "but voluntarily submitted to all the privations of poverty."[2]

This was true throughout his earthly pilgrimage. Jesus lived the simple life. In the years of his public ministry he did not have a regular income but depended on the charity of people (mainly women) who had a vision for his kingdom. Without a place to call his own, Jesus was homeless. His poverty continued all the way to the cross, where they took away his last scrap of clothing and nailed him to the cursed tree.

ENRICHMENT THROUGH IMPOVERISHMENT

Understand that Jesus did all this for you. Paul emphasizes this by saying that Jesus became poor "for your sake." Everything that Jesus ever did for the salvation of the world was done with a heart of love for *you*, the person reading this book.

When Jesus was born in a barn and was laid in a manger, he did it for you. When he was starving for bread in the wilderness, he did it for you. When he was homeless in Israel, like a fox without a den or a bird without a nest, he did it for you. And when he offered his life and his blood on the cross, in the poverty of his crucifixion, it was all for you.

But here is the best part: this costly provision of grace has made you rich beyond your wildest dreams. Follow the logic of this verse. A transfer of wealth has taken place in which God the Son has given his splendor away in order "that you by his poverty might become rich" (2 Cor. 8:9). His impoverishment is your enrichment.

I wish I had the words or the insight to give you a complete economic impact statement that would convey the full extent of your personal wealth in Jesus Christ. Remember that there was a time when you lived under a crushing load of spiritual debt. The Bible typically describes the guilt of our sin as something we owe to God—a debt so massive that we could never repay it out of our own resources. Anyone who has ever been in serious debt knows the sense of desperation that comes with owing more than you can possibly pay. But through his poverty the Son of God has canceled our debt. His infinitely precious blood has paid the full price of our sin.

Now we live in the hope of a vast inheritance. I reminded my old college roommate of this at a time of discouragement. As a starving artist, he was struggling to make it in the music world and was sometimes tempted to call it quits. I told him not to forget something that I sometimes find it hard to remember: as sons of the Most High God we are princes of an eternal kingdom.

In one of his radio monologues on *A Prairie Home Companion*, Garrison Keillor tells the story of a hard-luck family from Lake Wobegon, Minnesota. A nice young Swedish woman runs off with a Scotsman, a stranger by the name of Campbell. They have three children together, but eventually Campbell leaves, and his wife has to go home in disgrace. She and her three children live in an old, broken-down trailer, dependent on the charity of family and the pity of friends, always dreaming of a better life.

Then one day they get a letter asking for information about their family heritage, specifically their connection to the clan Campbell. Soon someone writes again to inform them that they are direct lineal descendants of the House of Stuart, the ancient and royal family of Scotland, and therefore rightful heirs to the throne. The letter closes with these words to the firstborn son:

> Your Royal Highness, discovering you and your family has been the happiest accomplishment of my life. And if God, in his infinite wisdom, should deny me the opportunity to meet you face to face on this earth, I should still count myself the luckiest of men for this chance—however small—to restore Scotland to her former greatness. Please know that you are in my thoughts and prayers every day, and that I will work with every ounce of my being to restore you from your sad exile to the lands, the goods and the reverence to which you, by the will of God are entitled.

This happy letter should remind us of our own inheritance. We too have received a message from a far place, assuring us that by virtue of our adoption in Christ, we belong to the royal house of God. Our Father in heaven has a plan to elevate us all to greatness. We are in his thoughts and prayers every day, and he is working with every ounce of his being to restore us from the sad exile of our sin to the glorious inheritance to which we are rightly entitled as the true children of God.

No matter what hardships we face in life, therefore, we have a royal identity. This is not merely a metaphor; it is the ultimate reality. Our royal standing as the sons and daughters of God comes with the promise of an everlasting inheritance: "The Spirit himself bears witness with our spirit that we are children of God, and if children, then heirs—heirs of God and fellow heirs with Christ" (Rom. 8:16–17). When we read what the Bible says about the coming of the kingdom of God, it is all mansions and crowns, with gold in the streets and glory streaming from the face of Jesus Christ.

The promise of such wealth puts our present experience into perspective. Here we are, stressed out by how much work we have to do, or worried about our finances, or obsessing over our bodies, or anxious about our families, or troubled by all the other troubles of life. All of these struggles have their place in life, but we should see them in the context of eternity. Someone who is about to come into possession of a vast fortune does not worry about a current shortfall. This should be our perspective as well: caring less about what we have or do not have in this life and hoping more in the glory that is waiting to be revealed in Jesus Christ, through the costly provision of his grace.

GIVING OURSELVES AWAY

Apparently, all of this is something we know already. This is clear from what Paul says at the beginning of the verse: "You know the grace of our Lord Jesus Christ." But the real point, of course, is not just to know this, but to live it out.

The context for what Paul says about the costly provision of God's grace is generous giving. As someone sensitive to suffering, he wanted to encourage the Corinthians to give generously to kingdom work and especially to care for poor believers. The apostle was sensitive to the plight of suffering Christians. He grounded his appeal to charity in the gospel, reminding the Corinthians that the self-imposed poverty of their Savior had made them unimaginably rich.

The application is obvious: we should spend our lives for the enrichment of others. God's costly provision of grace for us in Jesus Christ is a call to generous living. We are so rich—not simply in our possession of material goods, if we have them, but in our relationship with Jesus Christ and our expectation of an eternal inheritance. Meanwhile, billions of people are living in grinding poverty, not only materially but also, and especially, spiritually. They are living without Christ and without the hope of eternal life. How much of your life will you spend to make them truly rich?

Earlier I quoted Frank Houghton's hymn on the incarnation, "Thou Who Wast Rich." Houghton wrote this hymn following the 1934 martyrdom of John and Betty Stam in South Anhwei, China.[3] The Stams had dedicated their lives to sharing the gospel in a place that had never heard the gospel. In a sudden attack by communist bandits, they were taken captive and then brutally beheaded.

In the first hours of their captivity, John Stam managed to write a note that was later recovered: "My wife and myself are today in the hands of communist bandits. Whether we will be released or not no one knows. May God be magnified in our bodies, whether by life or by death."

Perhaps God will call us to make a similar sacrifice— or perhaps not. If he does, it will be an appropriate sacrifice, given everything that Jesus has sacrificed for us. With this in mind, we should always be ready to give whatever we have, up to and including our very lives.

3

GRACE'S JUSTIFYING RIGHTEOUSNESS

Some of the wisest people at any school are those who do the manual labor—the cleaners, repairers, and grounds-keepers. Consider what one of the physical plant workers at Wheaton College once told me about his experience of God's holiness, as he encountered it in the Bible. "When I open this book up," the man said, "I see that I'm so far from it."

What is your experience? Do you find that you are able to do what God says, or do you find that it is your very nature to go against him?

The Scripture says that "by works of the law no human being will be justified in his sight, since through the law comes knowledge of sin" (Rom. 3:20). When it says "no one" it means "no one": "*All* have sinned and fall short of the glory of God" (Rom. 3:23). But the Scripture goes on to say this: we "are justified by his grace as a gift, through the redemption that is in Christ Jesus" (Rom.

3:24). The grace we so desperately need has been generously provided at the costly price of the blood of God's only Son, and this gift of grace comes to us with justifying righteousness.

WHAT NOT TO WEAR

Earlier we saw that if we are honest about our true spiritual condition, we will say what the tax collector said when he prayed at the temple: "God, be mercy-seated to me, the sinner." If we do, we will have the same relationship with God that the tax collector had once he had prayed for mercy. Jesus said that the man went home "justified" in the sight of God.

But what does it mean to be justified? One of the best places to see this is in a strange story from the Old Testament:

> Then he showed me Joshua the high priest standing before the angel of the LORD, and Satan standing at his right hand to accuse him. And the LORD said to Satan, "The LORD rebuke you, O Satan! The LORD who has chosen Jerusalem rebuke you! Is not this a brand plucked from the fire?" Now Joshua was standing before the angel, clothed with filthy garments. And the angel said to those who were standing before him, "Remove the filthy garments from him." And to him he said, "Behold, I have taken your iniquity away from you, and I will clothe you with pure vestments." And I said, "Let them put a clean turban on his head." So they put a clean turban on

his head and clothed him with garments. And the angel of the LORD was standing by. (Zech. 3:1–5)

The way this story opens sounds like something from *What Not to Wear,* a television program that always begins with candid footage of a woman whose friends think she needs an entirely new wardrobe. Early in the show, the woman puts on one or two of her favorite outfits and walks into a room of brightly illuminated mirrors. With 360 degrees of reflection, there is no place to hide. Every flaw in her fashion and physique is exposed before a national television audience. What a nightmare! Then it gets worse, because two fashion consultants walk in to tell her exactly what they think about what she is wearing. Their critique is always caustic.

What Not to Wear is a modern-day parallel to the nightmare that Zechariah experienced. In his dream, the prophet witnessed Joshua the high priest standing before the Lord dressed in filthy clothes, with Satan standing by to accuse him.

To understand why this was such a nightmare, it helps to understand who Joshua was—not the famous general under Moses, but a man who lived many centuries later and served as Israel's high priest. Now, the high priest was supposed to be the holiest man in the world. It was his responsibility to go once a year into the Most Holy Place—the place where God was—and offer a blood sacrifice that would pay for all the sins of the people of God.

The priest had a dangerous job—a matter of life and death. On occasion, when priests entered the Most Holy Place without permission they were struck dead (e.g., Lev. 10:1–7). So the high priest had to be careful how he dressed. The law of Moses gave detailed instructions for his clothing, all the way down to his sacred underwear (see Ex. 28:43).

Needless to say, it was very important for these priestly vestments to be pristine! As he represented the people before God, the high priest was supposed to be covered in spotless holiness. This explains why Zechariah's dream was such a nightmare. He saw Joshua the high priest standing before God—not just at the temple but in the very courts of heaven. He was supposed to be absolutely spotless, but instead he was wearing filthy clothes.

The word the Bible uses to describe the condition of Joshua's garments is vulgar. It means "filth, specifically human excrement."[1] We have one or two similar words in the English language—words that should never be used in polite company. In short, Joshua the high priest was wearing "what not to wear."

Understand that Zechariah's dream is really a picture of our sin. The Bible often uses the imagery of clothing to describe our spiritual condition before God. This is especially true when the high priest is involved, because it was his job to represent people before God. So when Zechariah saw the high priest covered in filth, he was really seeing a picture of his people's sin, his own sin included.

Most of us are inclined to minimize our sin. We compare ourselves to others who seem to be more sinful than we are. "At least I'm not like her!" we say. Or we excuse our sin, claiming that it was justified in some way. Or we simply get used to our sin. But when we put our self-indulgence, self-advancement, and self-pity next to God, we are forced to admit that our sins are filthy in his sight.

THE ACCUSER

It gets worse. Not only was the high priest stained with his filthy sin, but Satan was standing there to accuse him. Anyone who knows what kind of clothes the high priest was supposed to wear, and how dangerous it was to enter God's holy sanctuary, would immediately recognize that Joshua is a dead man. According to God's own law, there was no way for a priest who looked like this to survive the holiness of God, especially with Satan standing there to say that he ought to be damned.

This story from the Old Testament captures what is really at stake in our justification. What will happen to us at the bar of God's justice? Will we be justified or condemned? Will we be damned or delivered? It is one thing to hope that God will find us righteous but another thing to know for sure.

To illustrate this point, consider the story of a man who thought he was good enough for God . . . until he discovered that he wasn't. It's a true story that made a huge impression on me when I heard it as a child: the story of Donald Smarto.

When he gives his testimony of faith in Jesus Christ, Smarto tells about the time when he was studying for the priesthood and was chosen to perform the role of a cardinal in a religious play. To look the part, the seminary arranged for him to borrow ornate robes from his local diocese. When they arrived, Smarto was excited to try them on. He went to his room, locked the door, and tried them on: a scarlet robe with a flowing cape.

Soon these vestments became an obsession. Although the play began at eight o'clock at night, Smarto found himself putting the robes on earlier and earlier in the day. By the last days of the performance, he was dressing in the mid-afternoon, strutting back and forth in front of the mirror and basking in his feeling of moral superiority. "I liked what I saw," Smarto testifies. "I had a sense that I was holy. I simply didn't think I was a sinner; I felt confident that my works pleased God."[2]

Yet Smarto's false confidence was totally shattered when he saw what the person under the robes was really like. It happened at the movies, when a bishop dressed in a beautiful garment, studded with sparkling gems, walked out slowly from behind a curtain. Suddenly a large gust of wind ripped open his robes, revealing a rotted skeleton underneath. Smarto writes:

> In an instant, my mind said, *That's me. That's me?* I immediately blocked out the thought. When *I* wore religious garments, it was not pretense! The film was no longer funny. . . . "That's not me!" I said. . . .

I wanted to push the film images out of my mind,
but it didn't work. I continued to feel as if somebody
had hit me in the head with a two-by-four. . . . I kept
talking to myself and to God to try to make myself
feel better. "Make this feeling go away," I said to
God. "I am *not* a hypocrite. I am *not* an actor. I'm a
good person!" I kept thinking of all the good things I
did, of the fasting and sacrifices and the long periods
of kneeling. I reminded God that I followed the law
to the letter and that I did it in his name. . . . Yet,
these thoughts didn't bring the consolation that they
had in the past.³

This is what happens when a Pharisee suddenly discovers
that he is really a tax collector: he knows that underneath
the showy facade, he is a desperate sinner.

WHAT TO WEAR
Before I finish the story and tell you what the aspiring
priest did next, I invite you to consider what you would
have done. What is the right thing to do when you discover that you are not the good person that you thought
you were? What do you do when you find out that your
soul is wearing "what not to wear?" What do you do when
the accusations come—the accusations of a guilty con-
science, or maybe of the Devil himself?

What people do on television is to provide a whole new
wardrobe. At least, this is what the fashion consultants
do on *What Not to Wear*. They throw all your old clothes
in the garbage and then send you to New York City on a

shopping spree. And if you still have trouble finding the right clothes, they step in to help.

This is more or less what happens in Zechariah 3. This is also where the story gets amazing, because God did not punish the high priest after all. Remember the nightmare: Joshua the high priest was standing before God in filthy clothes, with Satan there to accuse him. The man deserved to be damned.

Then God himself suddenly intervened, showing the life-changing grace of his forgiveness for sinners. God did this by removing Joshua's filthy clothes and replacing them with righteous robes: "The angel said to those who were standing before him, 'Take off his filthy clothes'" (Zech. 3:4). So they stripped the high priest down to his bare skin. As he stood there, naked and trembling with fear, the Lord said, "See, I have taken away your sin, and I will put rich garments on you" (Zech. 3:4 NIV).

The word "sin" is important, because it clarifies the symbolism of this story: the dirty clothes definitely stand for sin. But God did not just leave Joshua standing there, filthy in his sins. No, by his own initiative he took away Joshua's sins.

This shows us something important about God's life-changing grace. Many people believe that God is for good people, so you have to make yourself better before you can come to God. First you clean your life up; *then* God will accept you.

This is not how grace works. In fact, it is exactly the

opposite. God does not say, "Clean up and come," but "Come, and clean up." We see this in Zechariah's story. There was nothing Joshua could do to save himself. It was all by grace—the undeserved mercy of God. God accepted him. God took away his sin. God made him holy. And when God did this, the high priest was no longer covered with the odious guilt of his sin but was covered instead with God's own righteousness. "I will clothe you with pure vestments," God said (Zech. 3:4). And when he did this, Joshua was righteous in God's sight—not because of his own inherent righteousness but by the righteousness given to him as a gift from God.

Understand that this is a picture of the gospel. When Jesus died on the cross to take away our sin, he stripped away the filthy clothes of our unrighteousness. But that is not all that Jesus did for us: he also covered us with his righteousness so that we could be holy before God. This is what the Bible means when it says that Jesus *is* our righteousness (1 Cor. 1:30). Clothed in him, and covered with his righteousness, we are now good enough for God—not because of our own good works but because Jesus has given us what to wear: the gracious and life-changing gift of his own righteousness.

AT THE CROSS

Earlier I mentioned the shocking experience Don Smarto had when he discovered that underneath the proud robes of his outward righteousness there was a skeleton of sin. There is more to that story.

When Smarto returned to his seminary that night, he struggled to justify himself before God. He walked out into the surrounding fields to walk in the moonlight. Soon the moon was covered with clouds and the night turned black. As Smarto stumbled around in the darkness, with his heart pounding in fear, he cried out to God: "Tell me I am doing the right thing. Tell me that everything I do pleases you. Speak to me clearly!"

In the despair of his soul, Smarto heard a strange humming sound and walked toward it. He reached out in the darkness and touched a solid piece of wood. Of course! It was only a telephone pole. But as he looked up, the clouds began to part and he could see the crossbar that held up the phone lines. There, silhouetted against the moonlight, was the form of a cross. Don Smarto was standing at the foot of the cross, looking to Jesus for his salvation. Here is how he described the experience:

> Now I knew, I really knew, that Christ had died for me. It was coupled with the more important reve- lation that I was a sinner, that I was *not* the good person I had thought I was a moment before. All at once I embraced the telephone pole and began to cry. I must have hugged that piece of wood for nearly an hour. I could imagine Jesus nailed to this pole, blood dripping from his wounds. I felt as if the blood were dripping over me, cleansing me of my sin and unworthiness.[4]

I am not the good person I would like to think that I am, either. And neither are you. We are all covered with the filth of our sin. What we desperately need is someone to take away our sin and cover us with righteousness. That someone is Jesus Christ in all his life-changing grace. Jesus invites us to hold onto the cross, where he paid the full and costly price of our sin, so that we can be justified before God forever.

4

GRACE'S SANCTIFYING POWER

We usually think of the gospel as something that Christians understand and non-Christians don't, but Dietrich Bonhoeffer would beg to differ. In his little book *Life Together*, the German theologian and martyr describes the grace of the gospel as something that is very hard for religious people to understand. This is because usually we are not honest enough about our sin to see our need for grace. So Bonhoeffer tells it like it is:

> You are a sinner, a great, desperate sinner; now come, as the sinner that you are, to God who loves you. . . . God has come to you to save the sinner. Be glad! This message is liberation through truth. You can hide nothing from God. The mask you wear before men will do you no good before Him. He wants to see you as you are, He wants to be gracious to you. You do not have to go on lying to yourself and your brothers, as if you were without sin; you can dare to be a sinner.[1]

One of my goals for this little book is to persuade you

to take Bonhoeffer's dare and own your sin so that you can experience more of the costly, life-changing grace that God has provided for you in Jesus Christ. To that end, we have considered our humbling need for God's grace. We really are the sinners that the Bible says we are. If we are wise, we will confess that sin and pray: "God, be mercy-seated to me, the sinner."

We have also considered the righteousness that God gives to us in Jesus Christ. Our own good works are nothing more than filthy rags. Like the high priest in Zechariah's nightmare, we are wearing "what not to wear." But God has taken away our sin and covered us with the righteousness of Jesus Christ. In a word, we are justified.

That is not the end of the story, however. As we have seen, grace is not just the way *into* the Christian life; it is also the way *on in* the Christian life. So as we seek to live in a way that is pleasing to God, we never stop needing his mercy. We are called to a life of grace—a life of unmerited favor and undeserved blessing. This gift comes to us from the God who "saved us and called us to a holy calling, not because of our works but because of his . . . grace" (2 Tim. 1:9).

WHY WE SAY YES TO UNGODLINESS

The trouble is that even after we have been justified, we find it hard to say no to sin. In fact, we find it all too easy to say yes, because there are lots of things that encourage us to sin.

Let's start with an easy one: *sin can make you feel good*. Sin feeds on our desire to please ourselves, and every sin has its unique pleasures. Some of them are physical, like the buzz of chemical stimulants, or the sensations that come from sex, or the comforts of food. Other pleasures are emotional. Consider how good it feels to nurse a grudge, or how satisfying self-pity can be—the perverse pleasure that comes with feeling sorry for yourself.

Here is another reason to say yes to ungodliness: *the Devil tempts you to do it*. We are in a real spiritual battle. There are demons at work in the structures of society and in our own personal experience. Dark powers are striving to lead us into temptation. A little girl from my church in Philadelphia experienced this the day she was caught getting the cookie jar down from the top shelf. "Sometimes the Devil tempts me," she confessed to her mother, "and sometimes he tempts me good."

There is also the *sinful influence of others* to consider. If we spend most of our time with friends who use coarse language, or make sarcastic remarks about people outside our group, we will start to say yes to profanity and a prideful spirit.

Thinking more widely, there are all kinds of *pressures we face from society*, especially through media and entertainment. Honestly, when was the last time you watched a commercial that encouraged you to be content with what you have or a movie that made matrimony look sexier than adultery?

When it comes to sin, there are all kinds of reasons to say yes. The biggest reason of all is *our own sinful hearts.* There is something inside us—something we inherited from our first parents—that inclines us to sin.

Our fallen condition can be illustrated from the testimony of Two-Gun Crowley, who back in 1931 was one of America's "most wanted." Two-Gun had been charged with a string of brutal homicides, including a cop killing. When he was finally captured, after a fierce gun-battle in his girlfriend's apartment, the police found a blood-spattered note in his pocket. It said, "Under my coat is a weary heart, but a kind one, one that would do nobody any harm."[2] The man was in denial about his own depravity. To the bitter end, he insisted on the goodness of his heart.

The truth about Two-Gun Crowley is the sad truth about all of us: we have unkind hearts that sometimes *do* want to do somebody harm. The pleasures of sin, the temptations of the Devil, the sinful influence of friends, the pressures of society—all these things lead our sinful hearts to say yes to ungodliness.

THINGS THAT WON'T MAKE US SAY NO

Wouldn't you love to know how to say no to sin instead of yes? Isn't there at least one area of struggle where you know that you aren't where you ought to be and wish to God that you could make more spiritual progress?

According to Scripture, there is something that teaches us to say no to sin—something that trains us to renounce ungodliness and teaches us instead to live righteous and godly lives. In a moment, I will tell you what it is. But first I want to tell you what it's not, because you might be surprised to see what the Bible says has the power to teach us to say no to ungodliness.

It's not what most people think. It's not *the fear of getting caught*, for example. We might think that one of the best motivations for saying no to sin is that we will get in trouble if we do. The problem is that sometimes we go ahead and sin anyway. A close friend once asked me to pray for him because he was going on a trip and knew that when he went to the airport he would be tempted to buy gay pornography. I said, "Aren't you afraid that someone will see you?" "That's part of the excitement," he said. Instead of producing holiness in the heart, sometimes the fear of getting caught actually adds to the enticement of sin.

Here is something else that won't teach us to say no to ungodliness: *the law of God*. This claim would surprise many people. They would expect to read a Bible verse that goes something like this: "The law of God trains us to renounce ungodliness and worldly passions, and to live upright, and godly lives." After all, isn't that what the law of God is for? Isn't it supposed to teach us to be godly? Yet the law cannot change the human heart. As Paul explained to the Romans, the law cannot bring salvation because it is made powerless by our sinful nature (Rom. 8:3).

Living in a Christian community won't do it for us, either—even a community that is bound together by a covenant with God. Wheaton College is blessed to have a community covenant. In signing this covenant, every member of the campus community makes an annual promise to live according to biblical standards. The community covenant is a helpful description of what God requires in the Christian life and also of some things that may or may not be required—moral and spiritual judgment calls that we believe are wise for our community, even if they are not mandatory for all Christians. But in and of itself, no creed or covenant can train us to say no to ungodliness, because even if we want to keep it, there are times when our hearts will lead us far astray.

WHAT GRACE CAN DO

So I ask the question again: What has the power to teach us to say no to sin? Not the law of God, or the fear of getting caught, or living in the right community. All of these things have their place in the process of sanctification. To a certain extent they may help us in our struggle against sin. But the Bible says there is something else that we need.

We see the answer in Titus, which is a letter Paul wrote to the pastor of the first church on the island of Crete. There the apostle writes: "For the grace of God has appeared, bringing salvation for all people, training us to renounce ungodliness and worldly passions, and to live self-controlled, upright, and godly lives in the present age" (Titus 2:11–12).

It is grace—only grace—that has the power to teach us to say no to ungodliness and to renounce the sinful desires of this world, and to live instead a life that is pleasing to God. This is the sanctifying power of the grace of God.

When Paul says that this grace "has appeared," he is talking about the manifestation of salvation in the person and the work of Jesus Christ. The Greek word for *appearance* (*epephane*) means "to reveal or to make known." Paul is talking about an epiphany—something that has suddenly come to light.

The biblical word for *appearance* reminds me of the way that a college sophomore rescued me one summer up at leadership camp. We were staying in the Northwoods of Wisconsin at a camp where I have been going since childhood. I know my way around there pretty well, even in the dark, so I don't always carry a flashlight. But as I was walking back to my cabin on a black and moonless night, a college student with a headlamp rode by on a bicycle, skidded to a stop, and said, "Is that you, President Ryken?" Then he asked me if I needed any help and I said, "Actually, I do." The student had suddenly appeared to lead me home.

This is similar to what God has done for us in Jesus Christ. When the Son of God left behind the glories of heaven to become a man, his grace appeared like a bright and shining light to lead us out of spiritual darkness and bring us home to God. This has already happened. It "has appeared," Paul says, referring to a real event in human history. When Paul says this, he is talking not only about the incarnation but also about the totality of Christ's saving work. He is talking about everything that Jesus has done for our salvation: his birth in Bethlehem, his exile to Egypt, his upbringing in Galilee, his teaching and miracle working in Israel, and his going up to Jerusalem to be crucified, buried, and raised again before ascending to heaven.

The grace of God has appeared in the divine person and in the saving work of Jesus Christ. It has appeared for everyone—for all the kinds of people that Paul was writing to in this letter: free people and slaves, Jews and Gentiles.

God's grace is for everyone. So I want to ask you: has this grace appeared in your life? For me it appeared when I was a little boy. As soon as I was old enough to know anything, people were telling me that Jesus died for my sins on the cross. Maybe God's grace appeared to you a little later, when you were in high school and weren't even interested in spiritual things, or after college, when you were going the wrong way in life. Maybe God is showing himself to you right now. What I know for sure is that his grace has appeared to bring salvation to anyone and everyone who receives it by faith in Jesus Christ.

WHY GRACE CAN DO IT

When God's grace does appear, it will change your entire life. This was true for the people who first received these words from the apostle Paul. As I mentioned, Titus was the first pastor on the island of Crete. The Cretans were known for their ungodliness. In fact, the poet Epimenides famously said "All Cretans are liars" (see Titus 1:12). Epimenides came from the island himself, so he should know. The Cretans weren't just liars, either. Based on what Paul says to them in this letter, we infer that they were lazy, gluttonous, rebellious, loveless, argumentative sinners. In other words, they were more like us than we want to admit.

Yet the grace of Jesus Christ was doing something amazing in the lives of the Christians on Crete. It was teaching them to renounce ungodliness. Formerly they were practical atheists, living as if God did not even exist. They had been consumed by worldly desires and fleshly passions. But now they were starting to live righteously. Right now, in this present age, with all its evil temptations, they were learning to exercise self-control. Here Paul speaks about an ongoing work of grace—not just a once-and-for-all decision to follow Christ, but the continuing power to say no to sin.

How is grace able to have this sanctifying influence? What is it about God's grace that has the power to do what knowing God's law and living in Christian community do not have the power to do? These are deep questions that will repay further reflection, but here are a few answers to get us started.

Grace teaches us to say no to sin because *it always gives*

us another chance. If there were no grace, then as soon as we sinned we would be condemned. But grace is the favor of an undeserved mercy that comes to us again and again. Sometimes we are tempted to think that every time we sin—especially if it's something we've done before—God gets a little bit more disappointed with us, until finally he gives up on us altogether. We forget that God has enough grace to forgive us again by the power of the blood that Jesus shed on the cross. So when we sin, we do not need to give up. God will give us another chance to grow in godliness.

Perhaps there is an area of morality where we have really messed up in recent days. Or maybe we sinned in some major way a while ago, and deep down we know that we're still not where we ought to be spiritually. Sometimes when we sin it's all we can do to drag ourselves back to the cross. What we really ought to do instead is run to the cross for mercy and then get busy serving the Lord again. One of the ways that grace teaches us to say no to ungodliness is by giving us a place to go with our sin and then offering us another chance to grow.

Here is another reason why grace has the power to sanctify: *it makes us grateful*, which is the best motivator for godliness. If we go through life trying to earn something from God, it will wear us out. If somehow we manage to succeed in measuring up to what we think are God's standards, we will be proud of what we accomplish spiritually and look down on other people. If we fail, we will fall into despair. But if we know what God has done for us in Jesus Christ—the grace that forgives all our sin—then we will live for him out of gratitude for his grace. Holiness is not a prerequisite for salvation, as if God planned to save only people who were good enough for him already. Rather, it is the grateful response of people who have been forgiven.

Shortly after becoming president of Wheaton College, I told the *Chicago Tribune* that I wanted the school to be a "community of grace." Immediately the interviewer wanted to know if I planned to get rid of Wheaton's grading system. She assumed that if you're living by grace, then there aren't any standards. In fact, just the opposite is true, at least when it comes to sanctification. The more we know the grace that God has for us in Jesus Christ, the more we want to serve him. Grace makes us grateful in a way that leads to godliness.

Finally, grace teaches us to say no to sin because *it brings us into a personal relationship with a living Savior.* When Paul talks about the appearance of grace, he is talking about Jesus, the Sanctifier. Sanctification does not come by trying a little harder to do a little better in the Christian life. It comes by having more of Jesus in your life. In your struggle with sin, stop depending on what you can do and start depending on what only Jesus can do. By the truth of his Word, by the power of answered prayer, by the nourishment of the sacraments, through the work of his Spirit—in short, by his sanctifying grace—he will enable you to live a godly and righteous life.

5

GRACE'S
CLARIFYING PERSPECTIVE

Sometimes knowing how other people see you can help you see yourself the way you really are.

I was reminded of this when I sat down with the graphic design team that Wheaton College hired to redesign our admissions materials. We talked about our "view book"—the glossy publication that high school students (and their parents) flip through to learn more about a college and hopefully to decide they want to apply. I asked the design team about the challenges they thought they would face in producing the right publication. They said we needed to find a way to communicate what an excellent education we offer without coming across as arrogant.

Many of us face a similar challenge at the personal level. Wanting people to think the best of us, we try to present ourselves to the world in the best possible light. Yet most of us struggle with a deep sense of insecurity. Rather than feeling confident in our abilities, we live with the constant fear that we don't measure up, so God is not happy with us.

Sometimes we find it hard to trust in God. We lack a full awareness of his forgiveness of our sins and his direct personal involvement in our own life story. We struggle to find a sense of our identity and our worth in Christ. We don't want to live with things that are incomplete, so we can't wait for God to heal us. We have too little hope for the future.

As a result, we live somewhere between arrogance and alienation, between pride and despair. On the outside, we want people to think that we have it all together, so that is what we tell them and try to show them. But on the inside we struggle with as much pain and doubt as anyone.

These attitudes are intimately related—indeed, they are interconnected. The arrogance and the insecurity go together because they come from the same heart. Yet this is one of the places where the life-changing grace of God can help us, by giving us its clarifying perspective.

PAUL'S EXAMPLE

By now we are beginning to see that God's transforming grace helps us with absolutely everything in life. It satisfies our deep need for God and for his forgiveness. It motivates us to give our lives away to others. It puts us in a right standing with God and begins to transform us from the inside out.

Grace also clarifies our perspective on ourselves. The only thing that enables us to see ourselves the way we really are—the way that God wants us to see ourselves—is the grace he has for us in Jesus Christ. This perspective was Paul's hope for the Romans, as it is the Holy Spirit's hope for us: "For by the grace given to me I say to everyone among you not to think of himself more highly than he ought to think, but to think with sober judgment, each according to the measure of faith that God has assigned" (Rom. 12:3).

The people who have this perspective tend to be extraordinary. They have a remarkable combination of humility and boldness. On the one hand, they do not take themselves too seriously. They know that all of their gifts come from God, so they don't have to prove that they're any better than anyone else. At the same time, they are always ready to use their gifts with confidence, not worrying what other people think, but serving other people in love.

We see this amazing combination in the apostle Paul. No one had a deeper awareness of sin than Paul did. "The saying is trustworthy," he said, "that Christ Jesus came into the world to save sinners, of whom I am the foremost" (1 Tim. 1:15). As far as Paul was concerned, he was a bigger sinner than anyone else in the world. Like the tax collector in the story that Jesus told, he saw himself as "the" sinner. This kept him from thinking too highly of himself. He constantly saw his need for the grace of God.

At the same time, no one was bolder than Paul in proclaiming the gospel. His awareness of sin did not stop him from serving the Lord, as if he was too unworthy to do anything for Christ and his kingdom. Instead, Paul took exactly the opposite attitude: his personal experience of God's grace for him in Jesus Christ gave him the confidence to face every danger in sharing the gospel.

The man was absolutely fearless. Consider what happened to him in Ephesus. There was a silversmith there who was angry with Paul for preaching the gospel. The more people believed in Jesus, the less they worshiped idols, which was bad for business if you happened to be marketing metal images of the goddess Artemis.

One of the silversmiths in Ephesus organized his fellow-craftsmen for labor action against the Christian church. Soon the city's huge amphitheater was filled with thousands of angry Ephesians. It was an absolute mob scene. For two hours straight, they shouted, "Great is Artemis of the Ephesians!" (Acts 19:34). Yet the moment Paul heard what was going on at the amphitheater, he wanted to go there and preach the gospel. The situation was so dangerous that most people would have considered it a good time to get out of town. Yet to Paul, it seemed like a perfect witnessing opportunity.

The apostle Paul had an amazing combination of humility and boldness. On the one hand, he had such a crushing awareness of his sin that he thought of himself as "the chief of sinners" (1 Tim. 1:15 KJV). On the other hand, he had such absolute confidence in God that he was ready to go out and change the world by witnessing to the gospel of Jesus Christ. It was all because he had the clarifying perspective of the grace of God—the grace that first forgave his sins and then empowered him to preach forgiveness to other sinners.

FOR WORSE AND FOR BETTER

A Philadelphia pastor named Jack Miller used to say, "Cheer up! You're much worse than you think you are, but God's grace is greater than you can possibly imagine." This was Paul's attitude exactly. He had an awareness of his unworthiness that did not paralyze him, combined with an acceptance of his gifts that did not inflate him.

Do you have the same combination in your own life? Are you able to face up to your sin and weakness and failure without falling into despair? And are you able to achieve victory and have success without becoming proud?

There are good ways to test whether you have the clarifying perspective that comes from God's life-changing grace. One test is to ask how often you find yourself making comparisons, whether you do it out loud or only in your mind. Ask this question: Do I have the confidence in Christ to use my gifts and abilities without making any comparisons, or do I find myself thinking a lot about how I measure up?

Most of us make a lot of comparisons. Whether it is physical appearance, social popularity, musical talent, athletic prowess, academic success, career advancement, family accomplishments, ministry ability, or leadership influence, we find ourselves thinking about who is ahead of us and who is behind us. Frankly, some of us find it hard to be happy unless we're first. And then if we are first, we find it hard not to be proud of ourselves, at least a little bit.

Here is another test: Do I spend more time building other people up or tearing other people down? Sometimes it is hard for us to hear someone else get praised without letting their success or their reputation go unchallenged. As we listen to the words we speak and monitor our inward thoughts, we should consider how often we elevate other people and how often we deflate them.

These are two good ways to test whether we see ourselves the way God sees us. Do we have to prove ourselves over against other people, or can we lift them up instead? Are we able to support them and praise them, even when they surpass us in the same areas where we are tempted to find our own identity? A critical spirit is a sure sign of pride.

If these are areas where you struggle, then "Cheer up! You're much worse than you think. But God's grace is greater than you can imagine." Until we understand this, life is dominated by our insecurities. We will find it hard to praise anyone else with genuine joy and almost impossible to admit our own shortcomings for fear that they will crush our spirit.

There are many ways to cover this up. Some people do it by making jokes all the time, trying to hide the pain. Others make sarcastic remarks. Then there are those of us who keep overachieving. What we are really doing is running away from an honest look at ourselves that will help us see our deep need for grace and then liberate us to live for the glory of God.

PAUL'S SECRET

The only thing that will enable us to see ourselves the way we really are is the grace of God. Consider again what the Scripture says: "For by the grace given to me I say to everyone among you not to think of himself more highly than he ought to think, but to think with sober judgment, each according to the measure of faith that God has assigned" (Rom. 12:3).

This verse comes at the beginning of what might be considered the practical part of Romans. The whole book is practical, of course, but in chapter 12 Paul takes everything he has been saying about salvation in Christ and applies it to the Christian life. This is why the chapter begins with the word "therefore." Paul is moving from salvation to application. In view of God's grace for us in Jesus, how should we live?

In verses 1 and 2, Paul talks about giving ourselves to God as living sacrifices. In verse 4 and following he will go on to talk about giving ourselves to one another in the body of Christ and about using our gifts for ministry to serve other people. But to do all this in a way that really honors God—to give ourselves to God and to others—we have to know who we are.[1]

Otherwise, one of two things will happen—both of them bad. Either we will be arrogant about our gifts or else we will feel so unworthy that we will hold back from using them. Either we will succeed in ministry and forget how much we need God to accomplish anything at all or else we will fail in ministry and then doubt whether God can use someone like us to do the work of his kingdom.

What we need is the clarifying perspective that comes from God's transforming grace. So in verse 3 Paul gives us a secret that will save us a lot of trouble. He tells us not to think too highly of ourselves and not to think too lowly of ourselves, either. And he says that what gives us this clarifying perspective is the grace of God. Grace shows us our desperate need for God (keeping us humble) while at the same time showing us how much God loves us (keeping us hopeful). From this perspective, we see ourselves clearly as sinners who are saved by grace *and* who have the God-given power to make a difference in the world for Jesus Christ.

GET SERIOUS!

To drive this point home, it helps to see exactly what Paul says. He begins verse 3 with grace—the grace that he himself had received. In her book on this chapter, Marva Dawn defines this grace as "God's overflowing, infinitely wise love, freely given, though undeserved and never repayable."[2]

The particular aspect of undeserved grace that the Romans especially needed was something Paul had received and wanted them to receive as well: the grace to see themselves in proper perspective, not thinking too highly or too lowly of themselves.

At the end of the verse Paul says that having this perspective will take faith: ". . . according to the measure of faith that God has assigned." Faith in the grace of God enables us to see ourselves the way God sees us. Until we trust in God, we will never be totally honest about our sin, or if we are honest about it, we will never be confident that God still loves us.

This is an important insight, because it tells us what to do whenever we are struggling with pride or despair. In both cases we need to believe in Jesus more than ever. So Paul tells us to have faith in the grace of God.

The apostle also tells us to *think*. This is a little hard to see in most English translations, but various forms of the verb for thinking occur four times in this verse. Don't think of yourself this way, Paul says, but that way. Literally, "think with sober thinking." So seeing ourselves the way God sees us is not just a heart issue; it is also a mental exercise. We have to think about ourselves seriously.

The kind of thinking that Paul had in mind reminds me of the kind of thinking that Goldilocks did when she went to the house of the three bears. According to that old tale, when Goldilocks tried the furniture, some of it was too big, and some of it was too small, but some of it was "just right." Paul's approach to thinking about our gifts is similar: don't think of yourself too highly, or too lowly, but just right.

After all, thinking too lowly of ourselves—focusing on our failures and inadequacies—is just another form of self-centeredness. So be realistic. Use sober judgment. In that ongoing inner dialogue—in which sometimes you praise yourself and sometimes you condemn yourself—make a sensible assessment of who you are by the grace of God and what gifts you have to offer. Think of yourself as highly as God does: nothing more, nothing less.

Taking this perspective includes being realistic about our weakness, brokenness, and sin, but it also includes being realistic about the grace that God has for us, the love he shows to us, and the gifts he has given us. In his famous sermon on the "Weight of Glory," C. S. Lewis said that "to be loved by God, . . . delighted in as an artist delights in his work or a father in a son—it seems impossible, a weight or burden of glory which our thoughts can hardly sustain. But so it is."[3]

Knowing that God still loves us, no matter how messed up we are, brings deep joy. When we see ourselves as living under the Father's glorious love, it humbles all our pride and gives us the confidence to overcome every last insecurity.

A BALANCED VIEW

To explain the life-changing perspective that grace brings, here is how Marva Dawn summarizes the teaching of Romans 12:3:

The balance defined by this third verse is deter-
mined by the grace in which we stand and the grace
out of which Paul speaks. God's undeserved love
reminds us that we are nothing except for what
God does in and through and for us. Consequently,
we dare not think of ourselves more highly than
we ought, than we are compelled to think by what
the facts warrant. On the other hand, that same
grace also chose us, each of us uniquely, for special ministries within the community. Therefore,
we dare not think of ourselves more lowly than we
ought or our service will not be as effective as it
could be.[4]

One man who cultivated this balanced perspective
was a sixteenth-century monk named John of Landsberg.
Landsberg once wrote what he called "A Letter from Jesus
Christ to the Soul That Really Loves Him." If we are wise,
we will receive this letter as a word of counsel from an
older brother in Christ and as a message of grace from the
Savior who loves us and calls us to live for him:

> One thing I have to warn you of especially is your
> constant tendency to grow faint-hearted under the
> weight of your faults and oversights, and an inclina-
> tion almost to despair when a sudden lack of confi-
> dence reduces your firm decisions to nothing. I know
> those moods when you sit there utterly alone, eaten
> up with unhappiness, in a pure state of grief. You
> don't move towards Me but desperately imagine that
> everything you have ever done has been utterly lost
> and forgotten.

This near-despair and self-pity are actually a form of pride. What you think was a state of absolute security from which you've fallen was really trusting too much in your own strength and ability. Profound depression and perplexity often follow a loss of hope, when what really ails you is that things simply haven't happened as you expected or wanted. In fact, I don't want you to rely on your own strength and abilities and plans, but to distrust them and to distrust yourself, and to trust Me and no one else. As long as you rely on yourself you are bound to come to grief.

You still have a most important lesson to learn: Your own strength will no more help you to stand upright than propping yourself on a broken reed. You must not despair of Me. You may hope and trust in Me absolutely. My mercy is infinite.[5]

When we know God's life-changing grace, we see ourselves more the way that he sees us. This humbles our pride, overcomes our insecurity, and gives us such great hope in his infinite mercy that we are able to serve him fearlessly with everything we have.

6

GRACE'S PERPETUAL ABUNDANCE

There are two things we can do with everything that God has given to us—our time, our money, our abilities, and all our opportunities in life. Either we can keep them for ourselves or else we can give them away for Jesus.

To be honest, sometimes the temptation to keep things for ourselves is overwhelming. Rather than making time for someone in need, we surrender everything to the sovereignty of our own agenda. And rather than denying ourselves even one thing that we desire, we take care of ourselves first.

When we live this way, as we so often do, we are making a fundamental mistake. We are thinking only in terms of our own limited resources rather than trusting in God and his infinite supply of grace.

MR. SO-AND-SO'S MISTAKE

We see a sad example of failing to trust God's supply in a story from the Old Testament. At the beginning of the last chapter of Ruth, Boaz is a man on a mission. Against all expectation, the businessman from Bethlehem has an opportunity to buy a choice piece of land and with the land to marry one of the Bible's most beautiful women, in every important sense of the word *beautiful*.

Her name was Ruth. She was a poor girl from a far country, and because Boaz was related to her, he was in a position to help. But according to the biblical laws for kinship redemption, another relative had the right of first refusal—Mr. So-and-So, the Bible calls him (Ruth 4:1). So Boaz sat the man down in front of the town's elders and asked him, first of all, if he wanted to redeem the field. Mr. So-and-So said that he did.

Then Boaz turned the tables on the man. He explained that when Mr. So-and-So bought the field, the law would require him to marry Ruth. When he married Ruth, he would be obligated to raise a family with her, and this, in turn, would mean sharing his estate with her family as well as his own. When the man realized how much it would cost him to make this transaction, he quickly decided that he didn't want to do it after all. "I can't buy the field," he said to Boaz. "It would jeopardize my own inheritance. Here, you take it!" Which is exactly what Boaz did.

This story illustrates the selfish way that most of us operate most of the time. Mr. So-and-So was willing to give a little to get something in return, but he was so worried about losing what he had that he could not bring himself to make a costly sacrifice for someone else.

Most of us can relate. Often we serve the Lord with

what we have left over but hold back from making costly investments in the kingdom of God. To put this in economic terms, we give God only the interest of our lives, not the principal. For some reason we think that unless we hold on to what we have—our time, our talent, and our treasure—there will be nothing left for us.

WHAT WILL WE HAVE?

The gospel calls us instead to a more radical lifestyle of sacrifice. Consider the commitment that Jonathan Edwards made when he was a young man. America's greatest theologian was also one of the country's most radical disciples. Here is what Edwards wrote in his diary when he was nineteen years old:

> I have this day . . . been before God; and have given myself, all that I am and have to God, so that I am not, in any respect my own. . . . I have given myself clear away, and have not retained anything, as my own. I have been to God this morning, and told him that I gave myself *wholly* to him. I have given every power to him; so that for the future I will challenge or claim no right in myself, in any respect. I have expressly promised him, and do now promise almighty God, that by his grace I will not. . . . This I have done. And I pray God, for the sake of Christ, to look upon it as a self-dedication; and to receive me now as entirely his own, and deal with me in all respects as such; whether he afflicts me or prospers me, or whatever he pleases to do with me, who am his. Now, henceforth, I am not to act in any respect my own.[1]

There is only one thing that is able to sustain this kind of lifestyle, in which we keep offering everything to God, not holding anything back but giving it all to him. That one thing is the life-changing grace that God gives to us in perpetual abundance—what the apostle John called "grace upon grace" (John 1:16).

Earlier we considered the costly provision of God's grace to us in Jesus Christ, as proclaimed in 2 Corinthians 8:9: "For you know the grace of our Lord Jesus Christ, that though he was rich, yet for your sake he became poor; so that you by his poverty might become rich." This verse speaks of the glories that God the Son set aside to become a man and about our enrichment through his impoverishment.

The theme of grace comes up repeatedly in Paul's second letter to the Corinthians. The apostle wanted his brothers and sisters "to know . . . about the grace of God" (2 Cor. 8:1)—what he called the "surpassing grace of God" (2 Cor. 9:14) in Jesus Christ. Jesus has given everything for us. He died for our sins to grant us forgiveness. He opened the way to eternal life and has granted us the gift of his Spirit. Now he rightly calls us to give ourselves away for him.

We need to be honest about how hard this is for us to do. Our natural tendency is to be protective of our possessions, jealous of our time, and stingy with our money. Rather than living with a free and open hand, we often act as if there will be nothing left for us unless we keep it all for ourselves.

This attitude explains the wistful question that Peter asked when Jesus was talking to his disciples about how hard it was for rich people to enter the kingdom of God—harder, he said, than squeezing a dromedary through a darning needle, hump and all. Like the rest of the disciples, Peter was astonished by this. As he wrestled with the high cost of discipleship, he said to Jesus, "We have left everything and followed you. What then will we have?" (Matt. 19:27).

Sometimes we are tempted to ask the same question. We have made sacrifices to follow Jesus—at least they seem like sacrifices to us. We have rearranged our schedule, changed our lifestyle, and altered our spending habits. Sometimes we wonder what—if anything—will be left for us.

What we will find, however, is this: the more we give away for Jesus, the more he gives us everything we need. It is only when we give more than we think we can spare that we find out how generous God really is. Without exception, people who know to give for the glory of God are people who have experienced the extraordinary generosity of his grace.

GOD'S ABUNDANT SUPPLY

To understand how this works, it helps to know an important principle of the divine economy: the supply of God's grace is unlimited. In Paul's words, "God is able to make all grace abound to you, so that having all sufficiency in all things at all times, you may abound in every good work" (2 Cor. 9:8). Here the Bible speaks about a perpetually abundant grace that enables us to live an amazingly abundant life.

The context for Paul's statement about the super-abundance of God's grace is the offering that he was taking for poor people in Jerusalem. The apostle was writing to the Christians in Corinth, many of whom happened to be rich. Like a lot of rich people, they needed to be encouraged to live more generously. So Paul gave them an analogy from life on the farm: "Whoever sows sparingly will also reap sparingly, and whoever sows bountifully will also reap bountifully" (2 Cor. 9:6).

A wise farmer is not stingy with his seeds but sows as many as he can in the hope of an abundant harvest. Paul wanted the Corinthians to follow the same logic in giving their lives to kingdom work. The more they gave, the more they would get—not in the crass, material sense that God would increase their bank account but in the richer, spiritual sense that they would see what God was doing in the world and get to be a part of it.

My wife, Lisa, and I have experienced this for ourselves. Some years ago our church in Philadelphia started a capital campaign to strengthen our ministry to the city and support new missionary work overseas. Together we figured out the most that we thought we could give out of the resources we had. But a few days later Lisa told me that she wasn't comfortable with our decision. She believed we needed to leave more room for faith. In the end, we promised to give more than we were sure we could afford. And what we discovered, of course, was that God provided for all our needs. Just as importantly, greater generosity liberated us to live with less anxiety.

ALL GRACE

But don't just take my word for it. Consider again what the Scripture says: "God is able to make all grace abound to you, so that having all sufficiency in all things at all times, you may abound in every good work" (2 Cor. 9:8).

Here is a promise so expansive that you can build your entire life on it. The biblical languages do not have exclamation marks. Thus they use words alone—and especially the repetition of words—to indicate emphasis. We see this in 2 Corinthians 9:8, where various forms of the word *all* appear five different times, making the verse emphatic. Paul wants us to see the absolute abundance of God's grace, which gives us everything we need for every situation in life. "*All* grace," he says, "in *all* things, at *all* times, giving you *all* sufficiency for *all* good works." The apostle uses the same word a couple more times in verse 11, where he says, "You will be enriched in every way to be generous in every way."

Know this: God is able to give you "all grace." A person could spend a lifetime—no, an eternity—meditating on the full meaning of this phrase. "All grace" includes

God's grace to us as our creator: he brought us into being, knitting us together in our mother's womb, giving us the breath of life. "All grace" includes God's grace as our redeemer: by the blood that his Son shed on the cross he atoned for all our sin. We could go on to speak about God's grace in justification, in which he declares us righteous by faith, and about his grace in sanctification, in which the Holy Spirit makes us more like Christ so that we can become the women and men that we were always meant to be.

The point is that God is able to do all of this for us. John Bunyan testified to this in his spiritual autobiography. After God had rescued him from a life of profanity and depravity, Bunyan took the story of his life and called it *Grace Abounding to the Chief of Sinners*.[2] If we believe the gospel, then this is the story of our lives, too. God has made all of his grace abound to us in Jesus Christ.

ALL SUFFICIENCY

That is not all. Because of the perpetual abundance of God's grace, we always have everything we need. "All sufficiency," it says in some versions of 2 Corinthians 9:8. "All contentment," the phrase could also be translated, or "all that you need."

Do you believe that God has given you absolutely everything you need?

Honestly, most of us spend more time complaining

about what we don't have than thanking God for what we do have. Consider all the things that you have grumbled about this week, such as the job you wish you didn't have to do, the financial constraint you're under, or the physical limitation you have.

We gripe about a thousand little things every day. One good way to prove this is simply to keep a running list of all the grumpy remarks we make over the course of a single week. Then ask the question, "Is this any way for a person to talk who has received an absolute sufficiency of God's abundant grace?"

When will we learn to be content with what we have? Probably not until we learn that Jesus is enough for us, all by himself. As an example of the grateful way we ought to live, consider the testimony of one poor woman from the eighteenth century as she wrote about living alone in fellowship with a gracious God:

> I do not know when I have had happier times in my soul than when I have been sitting at work, with nothing before me but a candle and a white cloth, and hearing no sound but that of my own breath, with God in my soul and heaven in my eye. I rejoice in being exactly what I am—a creature capable of loving God, and who, as long as God lives, must be happy. I get up and look a while out the window. I gaze at the moon and stars, the work of an Almighty Hand. I think of the grandeur of the universe and then sit down and think myself one of the happiest beings in it.[3]

ALL THINGS, ALL THE TIME

For the follower of Christ, happy contentment ought to be an everyday reality. Notice what the Scripture says: "God is able to make all grace abound to you, so that you have all sufficiency *in all things at all times.*"

Again, this is opposite to the way that many of us think. Although we admit that there are some areas of life where God has really come through for us, we tend to focus on the things that he has not done for us, or is not doing right now. What we really believe is that he has given us a good deal of grace so that we have quite a bit of sufficiency for many things most of the time, but not all grace and all sufficiency for all things all the time.

As a result, a lot of our silent comments begin with the words "if only." "If only I could make the starting lineup." "If only I had a better complexion." "If only I had won the promotion." "If only I were not the victim of injustice." "If only my parents had a better relationship." "If only I had a more attentive husband [or a more encouraging wife]." These are just examples, of course. My point is not that those desires are wrong in themselves, but rather that it is wrong to suspend our satisfaction with God on their fulfillment. We need to learn how to listen for the "if only" statements that are robbing us of full contentment in Christ.

God's grace is sufficient for *all* things, not just some things. When Paul says this, he is not thinking exclusively about material possessions. His vocabulary is more expansive. He is talking about God's sufficiency for all things whatsoever. Furthermore, God's grace is sufficient all of the time, not just some of the time:

- His grace is sufficient in times of grief, when we have lost someone we love and need his comfort. We may tell him our sorrows.

- His grace is sufficient in times of poverty, when there is something we don't have but really need. He has promised his people daily bread.

- His grace is sufficient in times of struggle, when we are so stressed out that we're not sure how we can carry on. "Peace I leave with you," Jesus says, "my peace I give to you" (John 14:27).

- His grace is sufficient in times of uncertainty, when we're not sure what comes next in life and don't know how to figure it out. "I know the plans I have for you, declares the LORD, plans . . . to give you a future and a hope" (Jer. 29:11).

God's life-changing grace is sufficient for all things, all the time. If this is true, then we should trust him with all our needs and all our troubles. Whatever we are going through right now, we should know that there is not one time in life when God is unable to give us his abounding grace.

ALL GOOD WORKS

Once we learn to believe this, then his grace can flow through us and out of us and into the lives of others. The grace that God gives is not simply for our own benefit; it is given to us for the sake of others.

Earlier we learned that there are only two things we can do with everything that God has given to us: our time, our money, our abilities, and all our opportunities. Either we can keep them for ourselves or we can give them away for Jesus and use them to advance his kingdom.

It is easy to tell which side the apostle Paul was on from the way he ended this verse: "God is able to make all grace abound to you, so that having all sufficiency in all things at all times, *you may abound in every good work*" (2 Cor. 9:8).

Sometimes it is hard for us to abound in anything, let alone good works. We are wearied by the troubles of life and distracted by the culture around us. We get discouraged by the burdens of our work and disheartened by the brokenness of our relationships.

What we need is the grace of God, in its perpetual abundance. His grace is all-sufficient all the time, including today. By his life-changing grace we can keep on giving what he calls us to give and doing all the good things he has called us to do.

7

GRACE'S
PRECIOUS TESTIMONY

In his book *The Prodigal God*, pastor Tim Keller describes a conversation with a woman who attended his church in New York City. Like many Christians, she had grown up with a performance-based approach to the Christian life. She had always heard that God will only accept us if we lead a good, moral life. Now all of a sudden she was hearing that the way to get right with God is by his grace—not on the basis of anything that we do but only because of what Christ has done. The woman responded by saying, "*That* is a scary idea! Oh, it's good scary, but still scary."

Keller was intrigued. Christians usually talk about how *amazing* grace is. But here was somebody who was impressed with how *terrifying* grace is. So he asked her what was so frightening about God's unmerited, free grace. "If I was saved by my good works," the woman said, "then there would be a limit to what God could ask of me or put me through . . . . But if it is really true that I am a sinner saved by sheer grace—at God's infinite cost—then there's nothing he cannot ask of me."[1]

HOW PRECIOUS IS YOUR GOSPEL?

The perpetual abundance of God's costly grace calls us to a life of generous sacrifice. In particular, the grace of God in Jesus Christ compels us to give away the gospel to as many people as we can. Indeed, sharing the grace of God ought to be more precious to us than life itself. We know this from the example of the apostle Paul, who said in his farewell address to the elders of the church in Ephesus, "I do not account my life of any value nor as precious to myself, if only I may finish my course and the ministry that I received from the Lord Jesus, to testify to the gospel of the grace of God" (Acts 20:24).

When Paul said that proclaiming the gospel was precious to him, this was no idle boast. The man had proved it in his own ministry. Earlier in the same speech he reminded the Ephesian elders how he had dedicated his life to preaching them the gospel—everything they needed to know. He had taught in their homes. He had preached in their marketplace. He had reached across cultures, sharing the gospel with both Jews and Greeks. He had preached faith and repentance—the good news of salvation.

Paul did all of this evangelistic work "so that the grace that is reaching more and more people may cause thanksgiving to overflow to the glory of God" (2 Cor. 4:15 NIV). He also did it with little or no regard for his personal safety. In Acts 20:19 he refers to the trials that he had suffered in Ephesus—the same trials we considered back in chapter 5 when we looked at the apostle's rare combination of humility and courage. There were plots against his life, but Paul kept preaching. Through hardship and suffering, through shipwreck and storm, through prison and persecution—even attempted murder—Paul continued to proclaim the gospel of the grace of God. So what he said was true: he did not account his life of any value, or as precious to himself, if only he could do the one thing God had called him to do, which was to share the gospel.

As we consider Paul's example, it is wise to ask ourselves where evangelism ranks on our priority list. If we are honest, sometimes proclaiming the gospel isn't even precious enough for us to talk about spiritual things with a stranger on the bus, or to get personally involved with people at risk, or to share the gospel with an old friend who doesn't know Christ, or to turn off the computer for a few minutes and pray for the lost. Yet evangelism is a matter of life and death.

One missionary was reminded of the importance of evangelism after a terrible tsunami struck Japan in 2011, killing thousands. In a letter to friends back home in America he wrote, "What is tearing our hearts right now is knowing that 98 percent of the people washed away in the tsunami died without Christ."

The terrible fate of people who die without Christ and thus are lost forever compels us to consider the priority we place on sharing the gospel. Is reaching out to the lost with God's life-changing grace more precious to us

GRACE TRANSFORMING

than life itself? Honestly, where does it come on the list: right at the top, or somewhere after getting a better job, making more money, and having the family situation we always dreamed of?

One way to move the gospel higher up our list is to consider three reasons why proclaiming the gospel ought to be more precious to us than life itself. They all come from Acts 20:24—good reasons for Paul that ought to be good reasons for us.

GOD'S GOSPEL

To begin with, proclaiming the gospel is precious because God is precious. Here we need to notice precisely what Paul says. Details are important, especially in the Bible. As the Polish poet Czeslaw Milosz once noted, "When you've observed a detail, you must discover the detail of the detail."[2] The detail to notice here is that when Paul talks about the gospel, he calls it "the gospel of the grace of God." This is the only place in the Bible where we find this particular phrase, where we are told in so many words that the gospel of Jesus is the "of-God" gospel.

The gospel is precious, therefore, because it comes from almighty God. The supreme ruler of the universe, the majestic and sovereign God, the Lord of heaven and earth, the God of all nations, the triune Deity—this gospel is his gospel. What could be more precious than something that comes from the mighty and awesome God?

A university student once came to ask me some spiritual questions. A friend from a Christian college had given him a Bible over the summer. He started to read it and, also, to spend more time with Christian friends, learning about the gospel. As we talked, it quickly became apparent that the young man was almost ready to give his life to Christ. He had attended a retreat the previous weekend, and for the first time in his life, the Bible had come alive for him. "This is going to sound really strange," he said to me, "but we were reading Samuel and it actually seemed like God was speaking to me, that the Bible was relevant to my life."

I asked the university student if he was a Christian, but he said no, he had not repented of his sins or asked Jesus to be his Savior. So I asked him the obvious question: "What's holding you back?"

The student told me that he wasn't sure how to pray. His difficulty was not that he didn't know what words to use, as I had expected. No, his difficulty was knowing that if he prayed, he would have to acknowledge that God is really there, and if he acknowledged that, then God would have every right to take control of his entire life. The student understood what it meant to come to Christ. He knew that he was dealing directly with the living God.

This is one of the reasons why proclaiming the gospel is so precious. Because it is the gospel of God, when we proclaim it we are dealing with the ultimate spiritual reality. Proclaiming the gospel can never be just another item on our spiritual to-do list, therefore; it is the way we introduce people to the one true God.

In Acts 20:28 Paul emphasizes the connection between God and the gospel in a dramatic way. He reminds the elders of Ephesus that the people in their church were bought with God's very own blood. The apostle could just as well have said that they were bought with the blood of Jesus, which is the way the Bible usually speaks. But here it says that the church was purchased with the blood of God. This shows the great price that was paid for our redemption—it was nothing less than the blood of God. This is the costly investment that God has made to give you his life-changing grace. The blood on the cross was his very own blood.

I am reminded of this when I sit on the stage of Edman Chapel during worship services at Wheaton College. I look out and see one of the most beautiful sights in the world: the students that God has given me to love and serve. Then I consider how precious they are to God. Beyond all of their intellectual, artistic, and athletic abilities, and notwithstanding all their weakness and brokenness and sin, they are the blood-bought children of God, who shed his own blood for their sins.

This is one of the things that makes the gospel so precious. When people come to faith in Christ—as the university student I mentioned did just a few days later—they enter into a loving relationship with the God of the universe that will last for all eternity.

A GRACIOUS GOSPEL

The of-God gospel is also a gracious gospel, which is a second reason why it ought to be more precious to us than life itself. The gospel we share is the gospel of the *grace* of God. So proclaiming the gospel is precious because grace is precious.

When we say that the gospel is gracious, we mean that it is undeserved and unmerited. In the gospel God does for us what we cannot do for ourselves. We are dead spiritually, but God makes us alive. We are sinful, but God offers us forgiveness. We are unjustified, but God declares us righteous. We are unsanctified, but God makes us holy. We are mortal, but God raises us up to eternal life. It is by grace that we are regenerated, justified, and sanctified, and it is by grace that one day we will be glorified.

All of this grace is found in Jesus. His death gives us life; his cross atones for our sin; his righteousness justifies us; his Spirit sanctifies us; and the power of his empty tomb will bring us to glory. This is the gospel of the grace of God.

How precious this grace is for our salvation! John Newton said it well in his famous hymn on God's amazing grace: "How precious did that grace appear the hour I first believed!" But understand that grace is not just precious the hour we first believe; it has been precious every hour since we first came to Christ, and it will be precious every hour from now until eternity.

Such grace is too precious to keep to ourselves. It

needs to be shared! This can be illustrated from the story of an orphan from war-torn Liberia. During a time of civil war a group of refugees was fleeing Monrovia for the bush country. They happened upon a tiny baby tied to his mother's back. His mother was dead, but the child was still alive, so the people took him with them. None of them expected him to live, but he survived long enough to receive emergency assistance from the Red Cross.

The boy's rescuers called him "Survivor," and for the next few years he was passed from one person to another, until finally someone contacted an orphanage for help. The boy was five years old now, but no one had the resources to give him a decent education. After conducting some interviews and doing some medical testing, the head of the orphanage said he would come back in several days to take Survivor to his new home. The director kindly asked if the boy had a favorite toy he wanted to take with him. The old man who was looking after him said, "No, he doesn't have any toys, but I'm sure if someone gave him a toy, he would play with it!"

Soon the happy day came and Survivor went to live at the orphanage, toys and all. There he received a new name—not Survivor any more, but Benjamin, a biblical name which means "the son of my right hand." A few days later, there was another unexpected blessing. The president of Liberia was driving through the neighborhood with her entourage, and when she saw the orphanage she stopped to greet the children. So there Benjamin was—in his first week at his new home—shaking hands with the president.

This true story of God's grace is a parable of salvation. God finds us in our lost and helpless situation. When we are about to die, he rescues us and nurses us back to health. He brings us to a good home and gives us a new name. He settles us in a family and calls us his son or daughter.

There is more to this story, however. Survivor was very excited about going to the orphanage, and during the days when he was waiting for the director to come back and get him, he would run outside every time he heard the sound of an automobile and he would cry, "My people! My people!"

When I first heard this story, the boy's words struck a chord deep in my soul, because they reminded me of something that someone from our church had said a few years earlier. The orphanage in Liberia had been established through the support of Philadelphia's Tenth Presbyterian Church. A young woman from the church had been involved with the Liberia home through packing supplies to ship to the orphans. But it wasn't until the church's outreach pastor came back from Liberia that she really understood what God was doing. When she saw the orphans on the video she said, "Those are *our* children! God has given them to *us*. If we don't take care of them, no one will."

The reason little Benjamin could say, "My people! My

people!" was that there were people somewhere in the world—people whose lives had been touched by the grace of God—who said, "Our children! Our children!" This is what the gospel does when we share it: it touches people with God's precious grace in a way that changes their lives forever.

THE GOSPEL OF JESUS

There is a third reason why proclaiming the gospel ought to be more precious to us than life itself. It is God's gospel, it is a gracious gospel, and finally, it is a gospel that Jesus himself has called us to proclaim. Proclaiming the gospel is precious because Jesus is precious.

Notice that when Paul describes his ministry of proclamation, he calls it "the ministry that I received from the Lord Jesus" (Acts 20:24). Paul's calling as an apostle was given to him by the Lord Jesus Christ. His mission to the world was not his own initiative, therefore, but something he had received as a sacred and precious trust.

Admittedly, none of us is called to be an apostle to the Gentiles in quite the way Paul was. We have not had the same Damascus Road experience that Paul had, when he saw the risen Christ. Nevertheless, we have been called to proclaim the gospel to the world, and this calling comes from our Lord Christ.

This makes our lives and ministries desperately important. The Savior of the world has entrusted us with his precious gospel. If we know Christ, then we are one of his ambassadors or publicists. Therefore, we have a sacred calling in the name of Jesus to proclaim the gospel of the grace of God, no matter what the cost.

One woman who honored this calling at the cost of her own life was Elizabeth Freeman. After only seven years of service as a pioneer evangelist to India, Freeman was seized in a Muslim uprising, marched to a parade ground, and shot in cold blood. Earlier she had written these words to one of her nieces: "I hope you will be a missionary wherever your lot is cast, and as long as God spares your life; for it makes but little difference after all where we spend these few fleeting years, if they are only spent for the glory of God. Be assured there is nothing else worth living for."[3]

Sharing the gospel of God's life-changing grace was more precious to Elizabeth Freeman than life itself. So it should be for all of us. If we are followers of Christ, then he has a claim on our lives, and part of that claim is to proclaim his gospel to the end of our days.

This was Paul's ambition. He wasn't just thinking about what he would do next summer, or the year after that. He was thinking about serving God all the way to the end. So he said: "I do not account my life of any value nor as precious to myself, if only I may finish my course and the ministry that I received from the Lord Jesus, to testify to the gospel of the grace of God" (Acts 20:24).

We know that Paul finished his race and preached the gospel to the end of his days. What we don't know yet is how well *we* will finish. One thing is certain, however: the answer depends on what we think is truly precious in life.

Earlier I mentioned a capital campaign carried out at Philadelphia's Tenth Presbyterian Church. There were various projects the congregation was hoping to complete—some in Philadelphia and some around the world—but the primary goal was to grow in faith, prayer, and stewardship. A girl in sixth grade wrote to explain what she learned from giving to God's work:

> The children's capital campaign has shown me a lot about sacrifice. I have seen how working for God can bring me more joy than doing things for myself. When you spend an hour making cards for the church you can think of the joy that it is going to bring to the person who receives it, but after spending an hour playing video games you don't have anything to show for all your time—nothing that will give you joy when you are dying.[4]

This is a good criterion for anyone, at any age. Am I doing anything with my life today that will give me joy when I am dying?

Thinking logically, such joy is only possible for those who give their lives to something that is *more* precious than life itself. That something is the gracious, life-changing, God-given gospel of Jesus Christ, which we are called to proclaim to the world.

8

GRACE'S
ENDLESS KINDNESS

My friend found out he was sick right before Easter. To everyone's surprise, he had liver cancer—a death sentence, as it turned out. Just eight weeks later we laid him to rest with songs of praise, words of testimony, and many tears. He was a scholar, pastor, and mentor who for nearly thirty years had served as the senior minister of Philadelphia's Tenth Presbyterian Church: James Montgomery Boice.

Later we recognized how God had been preparing our pastor for this sudden departure. Over the last two years of his life, Dr. Boice had been putting his faith to music, writing new hymns of the Christian faith. Many of these songs focused in some way on the life to come.

One hymn was called "Alive in Christ." Dr. Boice started working on it shortly after he received his diagnosis. After he died, I realized that he had taken the words of Scripture—specifically Ephesians 2—and used them to give his personal testimony. It was a dying man's last testament of his faith in Jesus Christ.

Dr. Boice began his hymn with a confession: "I once was rebellious, corrupted by sin, pursuing the devil's dark path." He went on to talk about the way God had intervened by grace to give him new life in Christ. But I was startled by the third stanza. The hymn looked ahead to the future, praising God for resurrection life. As we sang, I could imagine my friend in glory, still giving praise:

> God lifted me up to the heavenly realms
> where seated with Christ I am free;
> In ages to come he will show me more grace—
> so great is his kindness to me.[1]

Consider what these words mean. However much grace God has shown to us in this life, he will show us even *more* in the life to come. Throughout the endless ages of eternity, he will show us the ever-increasing grace of his infinite love.

As I sang those words I wondered if they were true. Is it really the case that in the coming ages God will show us more of his life-changing grace?

It is certainly true that God's grace stretches all the way back to eternity past. His call to save us by grace is something he "gave us in Christ Jesus before the ages began" (2 Tim. 1:9). God is not just working things out as he goes along; his purpose is rooted in eternity. As John Stott once explained, "If we could trace the river of salvation to its source we must look right back beyond time to a past eternity."[2]

But does the grace of God also extend to eternity future? And if it does, is it extended to us in ever-increasing measure? I pulled out my Bible and turned to Ephesians 2. There I read that because of his great love for us, God "made us alive together with Christ" (v. 5) and "raised us up with him and seated us with him in the heavenly places" (v. 6). I also read why: "so that in the coming ages he might show the immeasurable riches of his grace in kindness toward us in Christ Jesus" (v. 7).

These true words from Scripture took my breath away. My friend had gone ahead of me to glory, where God was showing him more grace than ever. Some day the same thing will happen to me: in the coming ages God will show me more of his grace forever. I want you to have that joy as well, so I close this book by inviting you to consider the endless kindness of God's life-changing grace.

PAST GRACE

Ephesians 2 is full of the grace of God. This is where the Bible says, in so many words, "by grace you have been saved" (v. 5). It says this not only once, but twice, which is the biblical way of adding an exclamation point: "By grace you have been saved" (v. 8).

The Bible says this in response to our desperate need. As the chapter opens, we are "dead in our trespasses and sins"—not almost dead, or mostly dead, but actually dead. This verse reminds me of a letter I once received from a man who never fully understood the gospel until he sat beside his father's deathbed: "I was holding his hand when he took his final breath. . . . I did not call the nurse in for approximately twenty minutes. During that time I sat next to his body. There was absolutely no life in it and I was helpless to do anything to change that fact. I began to think about Ephesians 2. We were dead in transgressions and sin."

This is our true spiritual condition outside of Christ. In Ephesians 2 Paul goes on to describe what we were like before we gave our lives to Christ. In those days we followed "the prince of the power of the air" (v. 2)—Satan himself. We "lived in the passions of our flesh" (v. 3), following our selfish impulse for sinful pleasure. Worst of all, we were under God's wrath. Like the rest of the human race, we faced an eternity without Christ in the pains of hell under the justice of God. Our need for grace was desperate.

It was just at this point that God intervened. "But God," the Bible says, making a divine interruption. When we were dead, when we were following Satan, when we were living for foolish pleasure, when we were under God's wrath—right then the life-changing grace of God intervened to save us.

Some of us remember what it was like to live that old life of sin. We were going the wrong way instead of the right way. Even if we didn't fully understand it at the time, we were living against God, not for him. Others can hardly remember a time when we were *not* aware of the grace of God in the gospel of Jesus Christ. Yet when we look into our hearts and see all the sin that is still there, it is easy for us to imagine how much worse we would be if we didn't have Jesus.

What a difference it makes to know Jesus and his life-changing grace! When we were spiritually dead, God brought us to life, making us "alive together with Christ." When we were down, he lifted us up, raising us with Jesus. This is what the man who wrote me the letter realized as he sat beside his father's lifeless body at the hospital. He remembered the story of Jesus raising Lazarus from the dead, and for the first time he believed—really believed—in the absolute grace of God, who raises us up to spiritual life.

This is the grace we need so desperately that we cry out, "God, be merciful to me, the sinner." It is the grace that enables us to pour out our lives as a costly sacrifice to God. It is the grace that justifies, covering us with the righteousness of Christ, and the grace that sanctifies, teaching us to say no to ungodliness. It is the grace that helps us see ourselves the way we really are—the way God sees us. It is the grace that gives us everything we need so that we can do every good work that God wants us to do. When we understand how precious this grace is— how it can change a person's life forever—then we want to share it with everyone we can.

THE GRACE THAT LEADS US HOME

God's grace will be with us for the rest of our lives. This promise is memorably expressed in the well-known words of "Amazing Grace": "'Tis grace that brought me safe thus far, and grace will lead me home." After doing all the other things it does, grace will lead us home to God.

I was reminded of this in a beautiful way at the funeral service for the wife of one my colleagues. The service began with a beautiful rendition of "Poor Wayfaring Stranger," lovingly sung by the woman's daughter:

> I am a poor wayfaring stranger
> Wand'ring through this land of woe
> And there's no sickness, toil or danger
> In that bright world to which I go.

Then the refrain:

> I'm going home to see my father
> I'm going there no more to roam;
> I'm only going over Jordan
> I'm only going over home.

The journey continues in the second stanza. The singer knows that although dark clouds will gather around her, and the way will be steep and rough, she is pressing on to the beautiful fields of God. There a happy reunion awaits her. "I'm going there to meet my mother," she sang at the last refrain, her voice breaking with emotion as she grieved her mother's loss. "She said she'd meet me when I come / I'm only going over Jordan / I'm only going over . . ."

The final word never came. The young woman's heart

was too broken with grief to finish the song. But it was better that way, because each of us knew that the song brought us to "home." So we supplied the final word in our hearts, and as we did, we were reassured that God would do what he promised and bring us home to himself.

FUTURE GRACE

Going home is only the beginning, because there is more grace to come. The grace that leads us all the way through life and takes us home at the end will stay with us forever. So in the coming ages, when we sit with Jesus at the right hand of the Father, God will show us more and more of his infinite grace.

Consider at least four ways that this is true. First, in the coming ages, God will give us *a permanent home*. In this life we are pilgrims on a long journey—poor, wayfaring strangers, wandering far from our everlasting home. But Jesus promised that he would travel on ahead to prepare a place for us. He said that in his Father's house there are "many mansions" (John 14:2 KJV). My teacher promised me this when I was in kindergarten and first learned this verse. I've been longing for it ever since. Isn't everyone?

One way to catch a sense of our longing for home is to watch *Extreme Makeover: Home Edition*. In every episode of the television program, some caring, deserving family is down on its luck—often because of disease or disability. Their neighbors work with a local builder and a team of designers from the television company to build them a brand-new house. At the end of the show, when the family catches their first glimpse of their new home, they always break down in tears.

Every heart is longing for home. Sadly, in this life we never get there. Far from home, we often feel out of place. But in ages to come, God will give us more grace—the grace to be home, and home forever.

Second, God will give us *a perfect family*. Anyone who has ever lost a loved one to the cold hands of death knows how the heart aches to be reunited. I experience this ache every time I play golf and think of my father-in-law—one of the best men I know—who has gone ahead of me to glory.

Yet a day is coming when all God's children will be together again. At the coming of Christ, when the dead are raised imperishable, the Bible says that all believers will "share in the glory of our Lord Jesus Christ" (2 Thess. 2:14 NIV). Then we will be with our true, loving, perfect, and eternal family forever. The relationships broken by death and other difficulties will be healed and reconciled.

A powerful witness to this hope comes from the true story of the death of D. L. Moody. Over the course of the last day of his life, the great evangelist hovered between heaven and earth. He told the people at his bedside that God was calling him home, and that he was beginning to see the glory. "I have been beyond the gates of death," he said, "and to the very portals of Heaven." During the previous year the Moody family had lost two small grandchildren. So they were deeply touched when Moody suddenly cried out, "Dwight! Irene!—I see the children's faces!"[3] So it will be when we enter our own eternal rest: we will be home forever with the perfect family of God.

I call our heavenly family "perfect" because when we join that glorious company, God will give us *freedom forever from sin*. This is a third way he will show us more grace. In this life we enjoy the grace of forgiveness. We also experience the grace of holiness. In spite of our weakness, we are making spiritual progress, growing in grace. In the words of an old American spiritual, "I don't treat you like I used to, since I laid my burden down."

Yet we are still burdened by sin. There are little sins—such as complaining—that we don't think are all that serious. There are bigger sins that we keep around because we kind of enjoy them. There are sins that we hate but keep on committing anyway. We do what we shouldn't do (sins of commission), and we don't do what we should do (sins of omission).

One day we will be free from our struggle with sin; this is the promise of God. Saint Augustine said that when we were created, we were able to stand but also free to sin. Sadly, once we had fallen, we were not able not to sin. Yet God has given us this grace in Christ, that now by his Spirit we are able not to sin. But Augustine believed that in the coming ages God would show us more grace. Though we can hardly imagine it, a day is coming when we will not be able to sin.[4]

Someone once asked Joni Eareckson Tada what she was looking forward to the most about heaven. Joni is a quadriplegic who as a young woman was crippled in a diving accident, so one might expect her to say that she wants to walk, run, and swim again. But Joni said her deeper longing is to be free from sin:

> I can't wait to be clothed in righteousness. Without a trace of sin. True, it will be wonderful to stand, stretch, and reach to the sky, but it will be more wonderful to offer praise that is pure. I won't be crippled by distractions. Disabled by insincerity. I won't be handicapped by a ho-hum half-heartedness. My heart will join with yours and bubble over with effervescent adoration. We will finally be able to fellowship fully with the Father and the Son. For me, this will be the best part of heaven.[5]

FINAL GRACE

This brings us to the last and best grace that God will give us in the coming ages. It is a grace that no one on earth has yet been given: *the grace to see Jesus* with our own eyes and to gaze upon his beautiful face. The greatest glory of the new heavens and the new earth is the glory of the Lord Jesus Christ. And we are destined to see this glory for ourselves.

If we have true love for Christ, then some of our best experiences in life have come in worship, when we are so caught up in the praise of God that we leave behind every distraction and focus only on the rare beauty of the Son of God. In the ages to come, his glory will always be in view. This is the beatific vision that Dante wrote about in his *Paradiso*, and that all the great theologians have regarded as the highest possible blessing of humanity: to see "the light of the knowledge of the glory of God in the face of Jesus Christ" (2 Cor. 4:6). When we see Jesus in all his glory, we will know that God's promise to us was true: he will show us more and more grace forever.

Jonathan Edwards once preached a sermon on the joy of seeing the glory of Christ. The occasion was the funeral of the pioneer missionary David Brainerd. After a year of riding from camp to camp on horseback, more than a hundred Native Americans had been converted through the young man's evangelistic ministry. But Brainerd contracted a disease and died at the tender age of twenty-nine.

Edwards felt the loss deeply, not only for the cause of the gospel, but also because Brainerd was a close personal friend, who died in the Edwards home. Yet as Edwards delivered his friend's funeral sermon, his deep sadness gave way to abundant joy as he contemplated being with Christ in his coming glory:

> We cannot continue always in these earthly taber-
> nacles. . . . Our souls must soon leave them, and go
> into the eternal world. O, how infinitely great will
> be the privilege and happiness of those, who, at that
> time shall go to be with Christ in his glory . . . where
> he sits on the throne, as the King of angels, and the
> God of the universe; shining forth as the Sun of

> that world of glory;—there to dwell in the full, con-
> stant, and everlasting view of his beauty and bright-
> ness;—there most freely and intimately to converse
> with him, and fully to enjoy his love, as his friends
> and brothers; there to share with him in the infinite
> pleasure and joy which he has in the enjoyment of
> his Father . . . and to join with him in joyful songs of
> praise to his Father and our Father, to his God and
> our God forever and ever![6]

What I am trying to say, very simply, is this: God has
more grace for us in Jesus than we could ever imagine.
What I have written in these pages is only the tiniest
part of the life-changing grace of God, who has promised
"that in the coming ages" he will "show the immeasurable
riches of his grace in kindness toward us in Christ Jesus"
(Eph. 2:7).

God has grace for us in Jesus. He has grace for all
of us, in all our weakness and sin. He will show us that
grace today, and tomorrow, and every day for the rest
of our lives, until we reach our eternal home. And then,
after that, he will show us more and more grace forever.

At the end of his book *The Last Battle*, C. S. Lewis
describes the wonders that the Pevensie children saw
when they went "Farther up and farther in" to "the new
Narnia." Lewis closes with these words:

> The things that began to happen after that were so
> great and beautiful that I cannot write them. And
> for us this is the end of all the stories, and we can

most truly say that they all lived happily ever after. But for them it was only the beginning of the real story. All their life in this world and all their adventures in Narnia had only been the cover and the title page: now at last they were beginning Chapter One of the Great Story which no one on earth has read: which goes on forever: in which every chapter is better than the one before.[7]

So it will be for all the children of God. This life is only the cover and the title page of a story that will go on and on forever. By his infinite grace, God will show us his endless kindness, so that we may experience "what no eye has seen, nor ear heard, nor the heart of man imagined—what God has prepared for those who love him" (1 Cor. 2:9).

NOTES

Chapter 1: Grace's Humbling Necessity
    1. R. Kent Hughes, *Luke: That You May Know the Truth*, 2 vols. (Wheaton, IL: Crossway, 1998), 2:192.
    2. Charles H. Spurgeon, "Too Good to Be Saved!" *Metropolitan Tabernacle Pulpit* (Pasadena, TX: Pilgrim, 1977), 46:373.
    3. Dietrich Bonhoeffer, *Life Together*, trans. John W. Doberstein (New York: HarperCollins, 1954), 96–97.

Chapter 2: Grace's Costly Provision
    1. Hildegard of Bingen, as translated by Junius Johnson for Daniel Kellogg's anthem "O Greening Branch" (2010).
    2. Charles Hodge, *An Exposition of the First Epistle to the Corinthians* (London: Banner of Truth, 1964), 201.
    3. The story of John and Betty Stam is located at http://www.omf.org/omf/us/resources__1/omf_archives/china_inland_mission_stories/the_martyrdom_of_john_and_betty_stam.

Chapter 3: Grace's Justifying Righteousness
    1. "Tziim," Francis Brown, ed., with S. R. Driver and Charles A. Briggs, *The New Brown-Driver-Briggs-Gesenius Hebrew and English Lexicon* (Peabody, MA: Hendrickson, 1979), 844.
    2. Donald Smarto, *Pursued: A True Story of Crime, Faith, and Family* (Downers Grove, IL: InterVarsity, 1990), 105–6.
    3. Ibid., 119–20.
    4. Ibid., 122.

Chapter 4: Grace's Sanctifying Power
1. Dietrich Bonhoeffer, *Life Together*, trans. John W. Doberstein (New York: HarperCollins, 1954), 20.
2. Quoted in John MacArthur Jr., *The MacArthur New Testament Commentary, Matthew 1–7* (Chicago: Moody, 1985), 293.

Chapter 5: Grace's Clarifying Perspective
1. On the logic of Romans 12:1–8, see especially Marva J. Dawn, *Truly the Community* (Grand Rapids, MI: Eerdmans, 1997), 68.
2. Ibid., 66.
3. C. S. Lewis, *The Weight of Glory and Other Addresses* New York: (Touchstone, 1975), 34.
4. Dawn, *Truly the Community*, 69.
5. John of Landsberg (1555) as quoted by J. Ligon Duncan III at http://archive.constantcontact.com/fs059/1102478471821/archive/1103562501015.html.

Chapter 6: Grace's Perpetual Abundance
1. Jonathan Edwards, diary entry for January 12, 1723, in *The Works of President Edwards*, vol. 1 (London, 1817; repr. New York: Burt Franklin, 1968), 18.
2. John Bunyan, *Grace Abounding to the Chief of Sinners* (London: SCM Press, 1955).
3. Quoted in R. Kent Hughes, *Set Apart: Calling a Worldly Church to a Godly Life* (Wheaton, IL: Crossway, 2003), 40.

Chapter 7: Grace's Precious Testimony
1. Timothy Keller, *The Prodigal God* (New York: Riverhead, 2008), 121.
2. Czeslaw Milosz, quoted in Gregor Dallas, *1945: The War That Never Ended* (New Haven, CT: Yale University Press, 2005), 122.
3. Elizabeth Freeman, quoted in *The Voice of the Martyrs* (Sept. 2007), 11.

4. These words come from the written testimony of Julia Peterman.

Chapter 8: Grace's Endless Kindness

1. James Montgomery Boice and Paul Steven Jones, *Hymns for a Modern Reformation* (Philadelphia: Tenth Presbyterian Church, 2000), 25.

2. John R. W. Stott, *The Message of 2 Timothy*, Bible Speaks Today (Downers Grove, IL: InterVarsity, 1973), 35.

3. For two accounts of Moody's last day, see http://www. thehiddenmanna.org/?p=3087 and http://www.christianity.co. nz/life_death9.htm#_ftn25. See also Lyle Dorsett, *A Passion for Souls* (Chicago: Moody, 1997), 380–81.

4. Augustine, *De Correptione et Gratia*, ed. J. P. Migne, *Patrologiae Cursus Completus*, Series Latina, vol. 44 (Paris, 1863).

5. Joni Eareckson Tada, *Heaven—Your Real Home* (Grand Rapids, MI: Zondervan, 1995), 41.

6. Jonathan Edwards, *Jonathan Edwards: Representative Selections* (New York: Hill & Whang, 1935), 173–74.

7. C. S. Lewis, *The Last Battle* (London: Unwin, 1956), 183–84.

GENERAL INDEX

university student, 88–89; and the testimony of the physical plant worker at Wheaton College about his experience of God's holiness, 37; view of the students whom God has given him to love and serve, 90

sanctification, 59
Satan: as the accuser, 41; as the tempter, 51
self-righteousness, 17–18
sin, 40–41, 105. *See also* sin, things that won't make us say no to sin; sin, why we say yes to sin
sin, things that won't make us say no to sin: the fear of getting caught, 53; the law of God, 53; living in a Christian community, 54
sin, why we say yes to sin: others can have a sinful influence on us, 51; our own hearts are sinful; 52; Satan tempts us to sin;

51; sin can make us feel good, 51; society, especially through the media and entertainment, pressures us, 51
Smarto, Donald, 41–43, 45–46
Spurgeon, Charles H., 17
Stam, Betty, 35
Stam, John, 35
Stott, John R. W., 98
"Survivor's" story (a parable of salvation), 92–94

Tada, Joni Eareckson, 106
tax collectors, 16
Tenth Presbyterian Church (Philadelphia): capital campaign of, 78–79, 96; support of an orphanage in Liberia, 93
"Thou Who Wast Rich" (Houghton), 28–29, 34–35
Two-Gun Crowley, 52

"Weight of Glory" (Lewis), 70
What Not to Wear, 39, 43–44

SCRIPTURE INDEX

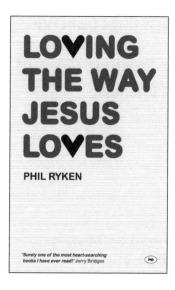

also by Phil Ryken

Loving the Way Jesus Loves
Phil Ryken

ISBN: 978-1-84474-565-4
224 pages, paperback

Most people are familiar with the 'love chapter' of the Bible, 1 Corinthians 13, yet Phil Ryken still has something new to say. He draws on the earthly life and ministry of Jesus to illustrate Paul's several statements about what love is and isn't. These aspects of love are then illuminated chronologically through the story of Christ's advent, teaching, miracle working, sufferings, crucifixion, death, resurrection and ascension.

Jesus never does anything without love. His love is everything the love chapter says that love should be. It is patient with sinners and kind to strangers. It does not envy or boast, but offers itself in humble service. It does not insist on its own way, but submits to the Father. It is able to forgive, trust, hope and persevere.

This approach highlights the crucial truth that we are able to love only because Christ first loved us in this particularly profound, very real, and transformative manner.

'Surely one of the most heart-searching books I have ever read.'
Jerry Bridges

Available from your local Christian bookshop or **www.thinkivp.com**

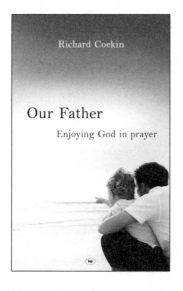

You Can Change

God's transforming power for our sinful behaviour and negative emotions
Tim Chester

ISBN: 978-1-84474-303-2
208 pages, paperback

You may be a new Christian, struggling to change the habits of your former way of life; an older Christian, feeling you've plateaued – you grew quickly when you first believed but now your Christian life is much of a muchness; a Christian who's fallen into sin in a big way and wondering how you'll ever get back on track.

Other books describe how we should live, but this book outlines how we can change. It's about hope: the hope we have in Jesus, hope for forgiveness, and hope for real and lasting change. God promises liberating grace and transforming power to his people.

Tim Chester points to Jesus and explains how faith in him can lead to change. Biblical, accessible and practical, this book also offers change projects for those who are serious about becoming more like Jesus and less like their old selves.

'A wonderful book for those who are serious about personal change.' Stephen Gaukroger

Inter-Varsity Press

For more information about IVP
and our publications visit
www.ivpbooks.com

Get regular updates at **ivpbooks.com/signup**
Find us on **facebook.com/ivpbooks**
Follow us on **twitter.com/ivpbookcentre**

Inter-Varsity Press, a company limited by guarantee registered in England and Wales, number 05202650. Registered office IVP Bookcentre, Norton Street, Nottingham NG7 3HR, United Kingdom. Registered charity number 1105757.